Health and
Wellbeing
for Muslims

Published by: Darussalam
                Unit 3 Estate Way,
                Leyton, London, E10 7JN
Tel: +44 208 539 4885
Web: www.darussalam.com

                Edited by Azhar Majothi
                Design and typesetting by Ihsaan Design
                www.ihsaandesign.com

Health and Wellbeing for Muslims

Action Plans to Help You Live Well

By Asmaa Ansari
(Author of *A Guide to Muslim Parenting*)

DARUSSALAM

Contents

Contents

Contents

1. Introduction

In the name of Allah the most Gracious, the most Merciful.

Verily, all praise is to Allah: we praise Him, seek His help, and ask for His forgiveness. We seek refuge in Allah from the evil of our own selves and from the evil of our own deeds. O Allah, send prayers and salutations on Muhammad, his family and his Companions. Whomsoever Allah guides none can lead astray, and whomsoever is led astray none can guide. And I bear witness that none has the right to be worshipped but Allah alone and that He has no partner, and I bear witness that Muhammad ﷺ is His slave and Messenger.

It is not difficult to notice that Britain's Muslims are often suffering poorer health when compared to people from the overall population. The observations are worrying and when I look around I see people not only in pain but also finding it difficult to cope with their illness and life's challenges. This is what has motivated me to write this book. As Muslims we need to not only look after our own health but we should be raising awareness of health matters and be actively reaching out to provide help and support in order to improve the wellbeing of the community:

The Messenger of Allah ﷺ said, *"The parable of the*

believers in their affection, mercy, and compassion for each other is that of a body. When any limb aches, the whole body reacts with sleeplessness and fever" (Sahih al-Bukhari 5665, Sahih Muslim 2586).

A number of factors are contributing to the prevalence of major diseases in the Muslim community. Poor diet, lack of exercise and stress are amongst the most prominent. All of these issues need to be addressed and of course medical treatment and intervention often has to be pursued in order to get better. At the same time we must remind ourselves that illness and adversity is a test for the believers which enables them to grow closer to Allah and there are many ways to cope with our difficulties and attain strength, patience (sabr) and inner peace.

This book will outline some of the strategies that can enhance our mental, physical and spiritual wellbeing.

Good health is one of the most precious gifts that Allah has given us. Islam emphasises the importance of maintaining good health and we as Muslims have been given the means to achieve this. We have been blessed with true and comprehensive guidance from Allah and His Messenger, the Prophet Muhammad ﷺ. Allah in His infinite mercy has blessed the world with His Holy Book and the Sunnah (traditions) of His Messenger as embodied in the Ahadith (narrations). Both the Quran and the Sunnah serve as Allah's mercy and guidance for us in all aspects of our lives including looking after our health and wellbeing. If we adhere to these teachings they will motivate us to adopt a healthy lifestyle and provide great benefits and ease for us in this life and the Hereafter.

My book is by no means exhaustive, nor is it a medical guide; there are plenty of those available in libraries and bookshops. In writing this book I simply wanted to share some of the information, tips and ideas that I have picked up in my quest to improve the health and wellbeing of myself, my family and others. The answers are in the Quran and Sunnah. Additionally I have included common sense techniques, like promoting good relationships and 'modern' approaches like the benefits of minimalizing and simplifying our lives. I have kept my book brief and simple as I am aware that in our busy lifestyles we do not have lots of spare time! I hope you will find some beneficial knowledge in it and incorporate some of the ideas and practices into your daily routines, In sha Allah. I pray Allah ta'ala accepts this humble effort in His court, makes it a means of salvation for all those who read it and continues to benefit me with it as a Sadaqah Jariyah after I have passed from this world. Ameen.

2. HEALTHY BODIES

HEALTHY EATING

Alhamdulilah in this day and age we are blessed to have an unlimited and unprecedented amount and variety of food available to us. Foods from all corners of the earth are in constant supply at the supermarkets and are just a fingertip away! However in order to maintain good health we need to be sensible in what we eat and Islam emphasises the importance of looking after our bodies.

We should not be excessive in our eating: we eat to sustain ourselves. At the same time it is important to eat a wide variety of foods to ensure that we are getting a balanced diet and that the body is receiving all the nutrients it needs.

In this short space it is impossible to discuss all the food types in detail so below is a brief overview of various foods and why it is important to include them in our diet.

Carbohydrates
Starchy carbohydrates should be included with each main meal as they are an important source of energy and provide fuel for the brain and muscles. Choose wholegrain varieties as they contain more fibre, and can help you feel full for longer. Examples include wholemeal bread and chappattis, whole-wheat pasta, brown rice and oats/barley.

Fruit and Veg
Studies have shown that populations with a high intake of fruit and vegetables have a lower incidence of heart disease, some cancers and other health problems. Fruit and vegetables provide the body with vitamins, minerals, fibre and carbohydrate, mainly in the form of sugars. Eat plenty of fruit and vegetables - the recommendation is five a day. Reach for a banana or apple as a mid-morning snack rather than a bar of chocolate. It is not difficult to toss together a salad or cook some vegetables to have with your meals.

Milk and Dairy Products
Milk and dairy products such as cheese and yoghurt are an important part of a person's diet. They are a great source of protein which helps the body grow and repair, and calcium is essential for healthy bones and teeth. Choose low-fat dairy foods as they are a healthier option.

Nuts and seeds

Nuts and seeds are extremely healthy and are a convenient and healthy snack to have between meals. They are one of the best sources of fat and also contain vitamins, minerals, protein and fibre. To give some examples:

- Almonds can lower cholesterol and help prevent cancer.
- Walnuts are good for the heart and brain.
- Sesame seeds can lower blood pressure and help protect against diseases like arthritis and osteoporosis.

Eggs

Although eggs have had some negative publicity in the past they are now recognised as being incredibly nutritious. They are an excellent source of protein, essential minerals and vitamins. They are also a rich supply of omega-3 fatty acids which help in the maintenance of brain function and vision.

Beans and pulses

Beans and pulses are an inexpensive, low-fat source of protein, vitamins and minerals. They contain fibre, and studies have shown that high intake of fibre can help reduce risk of heart disease and Type-2 Diabetes. They also count towards the recommended five daily portions of fruit and vegetables. Another bonus is that they are easy to prepare and keep well! Beans and pulses are commonly available in tins but they are more beneficial when freshly prepared. Note however that some need to be soaked overnight before cooking, e.g. chick peas and kidney beans.

Meat, Chicken and Fish

Meat chicken and fish are complete sources of protein which serve several important functions in the body including tissue growth and repair. They also contain vitamins and minerals such as iron. Red meat is higher in saturated fat so needs to be eaten sensibly. A healthier way to prepare meat is to combine it with vegetables, e.g. in a curry or a stir-fry. It is recommended that fish should be eaten at least twice a week, especially oily fish which is high in omega-3 fatty acids, e.g. salmon, trout and mackerel.

EXERCISE

Our bodies are an Amanah (trust) from Allah so we have a duty to look after our health. Good health is a blessing which can facilitate us in achieving great benefits in this life and the next life (Akhirah). Islam encourages us to look after our bodies and engage in exercise and sport, e.g. archery, swimming, and horse riding. The Prophet ﷺ and the Companions were hardworking and physically fit and he ﷺ advised his followers to be the same. A healthy body means we can worship Allah by fasting, performing salah and completing the Hajj (Pilgrimage) in the prescribed manner. We can also fulfil our duties towards our family such as raising children. Furthermore we are able to participate in voluntary good deeds like charitable work, visiting the sick, etc.

Exercise is essential both for our physical and mental wellbeing. It can help reduce the chances of developing major diseases such as cancer, heart disease and type-2 Diabetes. It can also enable us to maintain healthy joints and muscles thus keeping us physically fit. With lifestyles becoming more sedentary it is increasingly important to incorporate some movement into our lives. Whether it be walking, jogging, swimming or workouts, regular exercise is vital for a healthy lifestyle. The important thing is consistency;

> Remember everyone's body is different; what may be beneficial for someone may not work well for somebody else. If necessary seek medical advice before trying a new exercise.

develop an exercise habit that you enjoy and do it regularly. An example is HIIT (High Intensity Interval Training) which is a cardio vascular exercise that involves short bursts of intense activity with periods of recovery.

Leisure activities

An excellent way to stay fit, bond with the family and appreciate the beauty of Allah's creation is to go on walks with the family. This may be to a forest, hills or a coastal area. Local parks or commons are also great if there is limited time. The swings and climbing frames in the play area will always bring joy to children as well as helping them burn off excess energy. Combined with a tasty picnic, a trip to the park can also be a good way of meeting up with other family members or friends. Some parks have additional recreation facilities, e.g. "Banana Biking" or boating on the lake which can make a trip to the park more enjoyable.

Scouts

In recent years Muslim Scouting (including Beavers, Cubs and Explorers) has become increasingly popular to the point that there are now waiting lists for children who are interested in joining! The benefits of enlisting with a Scouts group are manifold. It provides

 a regular activity for children and youth where they can make friends, develop vital life skills like cooking and first-aid and keep fit with a variety of physical activities. Continual progress in achieving badges like the "Global Issues" badge or "Fire Safety" badge ensure that the scouts remain interested and engaged in their activities and events. Additionally the weekend camps which the Scouts attend develop independence and endurance and further reinforce their life skills.

An added benefit of attending Scouts is that young people can mention their learning experiences and achievements on their CV or UCAS (University Admission) form to give them an advantage in their application.

When combined with an Islamic ethos, Scouts sessions become a place where young people can benefit from short Islamic reminders, perform Salah (prayers) in congregation and learn the importance of having good manners towards others. Occasionally there are sponsored charity events, e.g. hikes which reflect the value of giving Sadaqah (charity) in Islam. Recently a local Scouts group raised money for young Dementia sufferers of a nearby hospital.

SLEEP

A good night's sleep is incredibly important for your health. In fact it is just as important as healthy eating and exercise. Adequate sleep can benefit your mental health, physical health, quality of life and safety. While we sleep the body repairs its tissues and the brain processes and stores information that it has received during the day. Sleep enhances mental alertness and a rested body will be more productive and creative.

Islam considers sleep as one of the signs of the greatness of Allah and it is a gift to mankind to enable us to rest and revive ourselves. Allah says *"And among His signs is your sleep by night and day, and your seeking of His Bounty. Verily, in that are indeed signs for a people who listen"* (Al Rum 30:23). For Muslims it is of tremendous value to establish a good sleep routine and sleep early so that we do not struggle to wake up for Fajr Salah or the voluntary night prayer (Tahajjud).

Tips for getting a good night's sleep

- Sleep at a regular time every day.
- Sleep early. This is recommended in the Sunnah and is beneficial for our heath and spirituality as it enables us to wake up earlier and take advantage of the morning hours.

- Avoid using your phones and devices in bed. The blue light emitted by screens on cell phones, computers and tablets restrains the production of melatonin, the hormone that controls your sleep/wake cycle. When you go to bed, keep your phone out of reach, preferably out of the bedroom, so you are not disturbed by alerts and notifications.

- Ensure you are not too hot or too cold.
- Warm milk with honey can often aid restful sleep. Avoid caffeine.
- Reading in bed can make you drowsy and help you to sleep.
- Always follow the Sunnah bed time routine:
  - Making wudu and lying down on the right side.
  - Reading Ayat ul-Kursi (Quran 2:255). The Prophet ﷺ said: *"When you are about to sleep recite Ayat ul-Kursi till the end of the verse for there will remain over you a protection from Allah and no devil will draw near to you until morning"* (Al-Bukhari).
  - Reciting "Subhanallah" 33 times, "Alhamdulillah" 33 times and "Allahu Akbar" 34 times (Al-Bukhari).
  - Similarly the Prophet ﷺ said *"Whoever recited the last two verses of Surah Al-Baqarah at night, those two verses shall be sufficient for him"* i.e. to protect him from harm (Al-Bukhari).
  - Reciting Surah An-Nas, Surah Al-Falaq and Surah Al-Ikhlas. Then blowing into the hands and wiping over the body starting with the head and face and then all parts of the body. This is to be repeated three times (Al- Bukhari).
  - There are many more Duas that can be read before sleeping. These can be found in pocket-books such as **Fortress of a Muslim.**

FASTING AND ITS HEALTH BENEFITS

Fasting diets are becoming universally popular as their advantages are being discovered. A number of studies have suggested that fasting can lead to numerous health benefits including weight loss, lower cholesterol levels and improved immunity. Weight loss can, in turn, result in better control of diabetes and reduced blood pressure.

Detoxification also occurs while we fast as any toxins stored in the body's fat are dissolved and flushed out of the body. During the first week of fasting higher levels of feel-good hormones (endorphins) are released by the body, resulting in improved alertness and a general feeling of mental wellbeing.

The fasting of Ramadan teaches us control and discipline in our eating habits. It is significant to note that the health benefits can only be expected if we avoid indulgence and overeating at the end of the fast. Too much emphasis on food distracts us and we lose the true blessings and benefits of Ramadan which is to bring us closer to Allah.

Food intake during Ramadan should be simple and not radically different from our normal diet. We should try to retain balance in our diet. Deep-fried food e.g. samosas and pakordas as well as sugary snacks seem to have become necessities in Ramadan but there are plenty of alternatives. Why not try baked spring rolls, light pasties, chickpea salad and a variety of fruit instead?

According to the Sunnah the fast should be broken with dates. These are an excellent source of natural sugar, vitamins, minerals and fibre. They provide instant energy, are easy on the stomach and aid digestion.

How to give charity on behalf of every joint of your body

The Prophet ﷺ said: *"In the morning, every single joint of yours must pay a Sadaqah (charity). Every 'SubhanAllah' is a Sadaqah, every 'Alhamdulillāh' is a Sadaqah, every 'La ilāha illa Allah' is a Sadaqah, every 'Allahu Akbar' is a Sadaqah, every commanding good is a Sadaqah, and every forbidding evil is a Sadaqah, and all this is accomplished through two rak'ahs one can pray at Duha"* (Muslim 720).

This hadith emphasizes one of the many virtues of performing Salat ul-Duha, a voluntary prayer in which two rak'ahs are sufficient as a charity on every joint in the body. It is also a means of gaining abundant reward and forgiveness from Allah. The time of Duha begins after the sun has fully risen and it ends approximately 15 minutes before Dhuhr prayer. It is preferable to offer Duha prayer when the sun's heat has become intense – midway between sunrise and Zuhr.

3. Purification of the Body and Wealth

PURIFICATION OF THE BODY

Cleanliness and purification is key to maintaining good health and wellbeing so Islam places great emphasis on it. The Quran states *"Truly Allah loves those who turn unto Him in repentance and loves those who purify themselves"* (2:222). Additionally our beloved Prophet ﷺ informed us that *"Cleanliness is half of faith"* (Sahih Muslim). Not only is cleanliness essential to protect us from becoming sick but it is also an important factor when interacting with others. Thus for example it is necessary to have a bath on Fridays so that the worshippers are clean and presentable for when they pray in congregation at the mosque (Jumuah Salah). There are other times when the ritual bath (Ghusl) is compulsory (Fard), e.g. at the end of a woman's monthly period, after a wet dream or after having intimate relations with one's spouse.

Complete and preferred method of having a bath (Ghusl)

- Make intention to purify oneself from impurity.
- Say "Bismillah" and wash the hands three times.
- Wash the private parts.
- Make wudu (see below).
- Pour water over the head three times, rubbing the hair to ensure that the water reaches the roots of the hair.
- Wash the body making sure that water reaches all parts, starting with the right side of the body and then the left. Rub to ensure that water reaches the entire body.

Purification after using the lavatory (Istinja) is necessary. This should be done by washing off the impurity with water; bidets found in many countries and douche shower-sprays are modern and convenient methods of achieving this.

Muslims are also required to maintain personal hygiene by ensuring that their bodies are kept clean and well groomed. The 'Sunan ul- Fitrah' are acts that are instinctive and in line with human nature. Allah chose these practices for his Prophets (peace be upon them) and we should follow them too. With regards to personal cleanliness five acts are considered from the Sunan-ul-Fitrah. Abu Hurairah ﷺ related that the Messenger of Allah ﷺ said: *"Five are the acts of Fitrah: circumcision, shaving pubic hair, clipping the moustache, cutting the nails and plucking the hair under the armpits"* (Al-Bukhari, Muslim and Ahmad).

It is preferred that unwanted hair is removed whenever it grows long, not exceeding a period of forty days.

Wudu (Ablution)

When a person wants to perform Salah (prayer) he needs to make wudu to remove minor impurities. This includes washing the hands, rinsing the mouth and nose, washing the face, washing the arms up to the elbows, wiping the head, washing the ears and the area behind the ears and washing the feet.

Virtues of Wudu

1) Expiation of sins

The Prophet ﷺ said: *"He who performs the wudu perfectly (i.e. according to the Sunnah), his sins will depart from his body, even from under his nails"* (Muslim).

2) The Believers will be recognized by their traces of wudu on the Day of Judgement

The Messenger of Allah ﷺ is reported to have said: *"On the Day of Resurrection, my followers (or Ummah) will be summoned 'Al-Ghurr Al-Muhajjalun' (shining and radiant) from the traces of making wudu'"* (Al-Bukhari and Muslim).

3) It is an act of sunnah

The Prophet ﷺ said *"Whenever you go to bed perform ablution like that for the prayer, lie or your right side and say: 'Allahumma aslamtu wajhi ilaika, wa fauwadtu amri ilaika wa aljatu zahri ilaika, raghbatan wa rahbatan ilaika, lamalja'a wa la manja minka illa ilaika. Amantu bikitabi kalladhi anzalta wa bi nabiyyikal-ladhi arsalta (O Allah! I surrender to You and entrust all my affairs to You and depend upon You for Your Blessings both with hope and fear of You.*

> This hadith explains the need to do ablution before going to bed along with the Dua. If we die the same night, we will die on faith and in a state of purification.

There is no fleeing from You, and there is no place of protection and safety except with You. O Allah! I believe in Your Book (the Quran) which You have revealed and in Your Prophet (Muhammad) whom You have sent).' Then if you die on that very night, you will die with faith (i.e. on the religion of Islam). Let the aforesaid words be your last utterance (before sleep)" (Al-Bukhari).

4) Saying the supplication after wudu is a means of entering Jannah

The Messenger of Allah ﷺ said, *"Whoever of you performs wudu carefully and then affirms: 'Ash-hadu an la ilaha illallahu wahdahu la sharika lahu, wa ash-hadu anna Muhammadan 'abduhu wa rasuluhu (I testify that there is no true god except Allah alone, who has no partners and that Muhammad ﷺ is His slave and Messenger)', the eight gates of Jannah are opened for him. He may enter through whichever of these gates he desires (to enter)"* (Muslim).

Miswak

Special attention should be given to cleaning the mouth as it is used for communicating with others. At the time of making wudu and at other times, e.g. upon awakening or before sleeping, Prophet Muhammad ﷺ recommended use of the Miswak (tooth-stick): *"The tooth-stick is cleansing for the mouth and pleasing to the Lord"* (Al-Bukhaari).

The Miswaak comes from the 'Araak' tree and research has established that it has active ingredients which promote stronger teeth and good oral hygiene. Also, by using it we will get the reward of following the Sunnah of our beloved Prophet ﷺ.

Perfume

The significance of a clean and pleasant body is illustrated in the Prophet's ﷺ love of perfume. He was known to have his own natural fragrance which preceded him wherever he went and remained after he had left. Nevertheless he still liked wearing perfume and recommended its use especially before  Friday prayer. He never refused perfume if it was gifted to him: Anas said *"The Prophet ﷺ would not refuse perfume"* (Al Bukhari).

Chapter 3

Chapter 3

PURIFICATION OF WEALTH

Zakat

The word Zakat means 'to purify'. Allah Almighty mentions in the Quran: **"Take from their wealth so that you might purify and sanctify them"** (9:103). Zakat is one of the five pillars of Islam. Allah has made it obligatory on Muslims in order to protect and purify our wealth. It is paid to the poor and needy in society. Zakat is payable if the amount of wealth you have owned for one year exceeds the Nisab. The Nisab is the market value of three ounces of gold or 21 ounces of silver. Assets to include in your Zakat calculations are cash (in hand, in bank accounts or money lent to someone), gold and silver, stocks and shares and money from property investment. Once these have been calculated Zakat is payable at a rate of 2.5% of the total value of your assets.

Zakat is the economic process for establishing social equality, ensuring that the very poorest of society are protected from hunger and insecurity and are able to buy basic essentials. Giving Zakat increases our sympathy and compassion for the poor and needy; it purifies the heart from selfishness and greed of materialistic products of the world. At the same time it removes feelings of jealousy and hatred instead instilling compassion, good will and brotherhood. It reminds us that everything we own belongs to Allah. We give Zakat to earn his favour and He rewards us abundantly for it:

"The example of those who spend their wealth in the way of Allah is like that of a grain of corn that sprouts seven ears, and in every ear there are a hundred grains. Thus Allah multiplies the action of whomsoever He wills. Allah is All-embracing (with his mercy), All-Knowing" (2:261).

Sadaqah

In addition to the compulsory payment of Zakat, Muslims are encouraged to make voluntary donations to help the poor and needy. This is known as Sadaqah and is also highly rewarded by Allah (see Chapter 10).

A Supplication to Remember

One of the beautiful Duas that Prophet Muhammad ﷺ taught us connecting spirituality and cleanliness is the following:

اللهم باعد بيني وبين خطاياي كما باعدت بين المشرق والمغرب. اللهم نقني من ذنوبي وخطاياي كما ينقى الثوب الأبيض من الدنس. اللهم اغسلني من خطاياي بالماء والثلج والبرد

"O Allah, distance me from my sins just as You have distanced The East from The West. O Allah, purify me of my sins as a white robe is purified of filth. O Allah, cleanse me of my sins with snow, water, and ice" (Al-Bukhari and Muslim).

Chapter 3

4. Mental Wellbeing

Mental health covers our psychological, emotional and social wellbeing. It affects how we interact with others, the decisions we make and how we handle stress. We know that stress can lead to mental illness but research is showing that people who suffer chronic stress are also at greater risk of developing major diseases such as cancer, diabetes, heart disease and ulcers. Thus it is vital that as well as looking after our physical health we should also pay attention to our mental wellbeing. There are many things we can do to look after ourselves and get the most from life.

> In our fast-paced society we can all benefit from increasing our resilience to stress and maintaining a clearer mind.

CONNECT WITH PEOPLE

Loneliness is a common cause of anxiety and depression so connecting more with people (not just online) is essential. Smartphones, computers and other devices are all useful for staying in touch and sharing information. But too much time spent on them comes at a price. Our minds need time, unplugged, to devote to family and friends. We are social creatures and our connections to others are key to our happiness and success. Being with people we care about creates feelings of warmth, closeness, comfort and relaxation. The closer the relationships the more benefits we derive from each other including shared experiences, help and support. Spending time with people is also a source of gaining Allah's love as the Prophet ﷺ was reported to have said *"Allah Almighty said 'My love is assured for those who love each other for my sake, who visit each other for my sake and who spend on each other for my sake'"* (Musnad Ahmad, 21525). In our fast-paced society we can all benefit from increasing our resilience to stress and maintaining a clearer mind. There are many things we can do to look after ourselves and get the most from life.

ELIMINATE NEGATIVE SELF-TALK

Self-talk is our "inner voice" which tells us how we are feeling about ourselves, and the situations we are in. When self-talk becomes negative we develop feelings of self-criticism, self-pity and self-blame. So for example we tell ourselves "I'm a failure", "I'll never be able to do this" or "It's all my fault…"

We know that Shaytan (Satan) is our enemy who makes us procrastinate, creates obstacles and makes us feel unconfident about completing tasks. He is **"The one who whispers into the** chests of mankind" (Quran 114:5). He introduces negative thoughts (waswas) into our minds and the nafs continues to entertain these thoughts. When this negative self-talk becomes constant and unrelenting it leads to anxiety, apathy and inability to function properly.

To overcome these negative thoughts/waswas our self-talk needs to be gentle and comforting rather than harsh and judgemental. We should develop a positive mind-set, have hope in Allah and make Dua for Him to empower us and give us strength. We should seek refuge in Allah from Shaytan and practise recitation of Quran and Dhikr, for "Indeed in the remembrance of Allah do hearts find rest" (Quran 13:28).

DEVELOP A POSITIVE MIND-SET

Positive Attitude

Difficult times will occur throughout our lives but it is up to us how we interpret them. Some people will feel defeated. They will wallow in self-pity or blame others for their misfortune, and they will not be able to move forward. Others will rise to the challenge and see their adversity as a test or a valuable lesson:

> At the end of the day it is how we respond to our circumstances that matters. It doesn't matter what is happening. What is important is how we respond and this is what determines our peace of mind and wellbeing.

they will overcome their hardship and even thrive.

In modern life stress and anxiety are common experiences for most people. Often there is not much we can do about the stress factors; we cannot change the past, or the fact that people will behave in a particular way. But we do have control over how we react to situations. We should learn to differentiate between what is in our control and what is not. Only then can we focus our energy on seeking solutions and quit worrying over events which are beyond our control.

Tawakkul

Tawakkul is trust and reliance on Allah. We need to have complete Tawakkul in Allah for in the Quran we are told: "And He will provide him from (sources) he never could imagine. And whosoever puts his trust in Allah, then He will suffice him. Verily, Allah will accomplish his purpose. Indeed Allah has set a measure for all things" (65:3).

From this verse we learn that we should always trust in Allah because He is our Sustainer. He will protect us and guide us through our difficult times. We need to rely on Allah because He is the Creator and Master of the Universe and nothing can happen without His permission.

Benefits of Tawakkul

1. Tawakkul leads to peace of mind. It teaches us to not be disappointed by what we have failed to achieve or acquire because we know that there is khair (good) in everything and Allah has

made the best plans for us.

2. Tawakkul gives us strength to face challenges and struggles in life while depending on Allah to take care of all our affairs.

3. We attain Sabr (patience) through Tawakkul. No matter what difficulty or hardship we come across, we remain patient and believe that whatever is happening is by the will of Allah and cannot be opposed. The mercy of Allah is shown in the Quran when He states *"On no soul does Allah place a burden greater than it can bear"* (2:286) and we are assured that a time will come when the test He is putting us through will end, for *"After every hardship there is ease"* (Quran 94:5).

4. The beauty of Tawakkul is that it enables us to accept every situation for the sake of Allah, This is illustrated in a hadith narrated by Muslim (2999) in which our beloved Prophet ﷺ once smiled and commented: *"How wonderful is the affair of the believer, for his affairs are all good, and this applies to no one but the believer. If something good happens to him, he is thankful for it and that is good for him. If something bad happens to him, he bears it with patience and that is good for him."*

Contentment

Islam teaches us to be content and this involves appreciating what we have rather than focusing on the things that we don't have. In the modern world we are constantly searching for ways to feel good especially by acquiring materialistic goods, e.g. we dream that "If only I could have 'x', I would feel better." We also practise deferred happiness, e.g. we tell ourselves:

"When the kids get older, I will do…" We need to live in the present and make the most of everything we have been blessed with. To ensure our wellbeing it is important to be content and to enjoy the journey of life rather than always looking to the future, regretting the past or wishing things were different. Being content is a sign of success as the Prophet ﷺ gave us glad tidings when he stated *"He has succeeded who embraces Islam, whose provision is sufficient, and who is content with what Allah has given him"* (Muslim 1054).

Gratitude

Gratitude gives us a sense of wellbeing and satisfaction and helps us appreciate all the blessings we have been given. It also makes us more productive and contributes to our success. By interviewing highly successful people it has been found that one of their daily practices is to wake up each morning feeling immensely grateful. This has led them to work hard and maximise their potential. Being grateful heightens our positivity and ensures that we are able to move forward even when faced with adversity. It is a quality favoured by Allah and is a means to gain His pleasure.

A Muslim should regard both good times and difficult times as a test from Allah: we should be grateful for His favours and we should be patient when His favours are withdrawn. Being grateful to Allah also results in an increase of His blessings.

SEEK HELP

Sometimes the difficult thoughts and emotions you are experiencing reach the point where they are uncontrollable and having a big impact on everyday life. If you, or someone in your family, is in this situation it is reassuring to know that there is help available and you should consider talking to someone, e.g. your GP, a therapist or a counsellor.

Some hacks to keep the brain healthy

- In the same way that physical exercise is good for the body, mental exercise is beneficial for the brain. Keep working your brain by trying to figure out things for yourself rather than immediately asking for help.

- Don't worry! It destroys brain cells and increases stress. As mentioned above think positive and put your trust in Allah.

- Don't dwell. Churning something over in the mind does nothing for our wellbeing.

- Learn a new skill. For example, using the Internet or learning Arabic/Tajweed (correct pronunciation of the Quran). There are a variety of courses available online or at local colleges.

- Develop a good sleep routine including a nap in the day. Muhammad ﷺ and his Companions were in the habit of taking a short nap or "Qailulah" in the afternoons. Studies have now shown that this is beneficial to the brain and boosts productivity by making you more alert and rejuvenated. It also enhances the memory and relaxes the mind. The benefits of a Qailulah are optimised when it is kept short so that you are still in the light stage of sleep and will be able to wake up without feeling drowsy.

- Practise memorising – especially verses of the Quran. This improves brain function.
- Crowd out negative thoughts with positive ones.
- For the respected elders in our community it is important to plan for your retirement so you don't find yourself waking up one day with nothing to do. Keep your mind stimulated to fight dementia. It has been found that participating in social activities, playing games and doing something creative can lower the risk of mental decline in the elderly.
- Try to remain focused. Concentrate on the job you are doing or the conversation you are having without being distracted. An example of being focused is developing Khushoo (sincerity) in our Salah and this attentiveness will benefit us greatly.
- As well as being good for your physical wellbeing, taking part in exercise is also good for the mind. During physical exercise the chemical serotonin is released in the brain which improves mood and can protect against mental health disorders. Exercise can help you feel less anxious and stressed as well as promoting better sleep. Joining a fitness class can be a way of meeting other people and making friends too.
- Drink plenty of water and eat a balanced diet as well as foods that are particularly good for the brain, e.g. oily fish and nuts (see Chapter 1).

5. Spiritual Wellbeing

Islam provides us with amazing acts of worship which not only enable us to gain the pleasure of Allah and achieve success in the Duniya and Akhirah but also contribute significantly to our spiritual wellbeing. Reciting and pondering on the Holy Quran, Making Dua (supplication to Allah), Repentance, Performing Salah (Prayer) and Dhikr (Remembrance of Allah) are some of the most virtuous acts of worship. Let us look at each one in turn and discover how they contribute to our wellbeing.

THE NOBLE QURAN

The Quran is the fourth and last sacred Book of Almighty Allah. It was revealed to Prophet Muhammad ﷺ and contains guidance on all aspects of our lives. Allah says about the Quran: "This is the Book (the Quran), whereof there is no doubt, guidance to those who are Al- Muttaqoon (the pious)" (Quran: 2:2). Reciting and reflecting on the book of Allah, and devoting regular time to its study, memorization and implementation has amazing benefits for us in this life and the next.

Blessings and Benefits of the Quran

The Quran gives us peace and tranquillity, as well as being a source of healing (see Chapter 11).

1. The Quran will be a proof for or against us on the day of judgement

This is due to the statement of the Messenger ﷺ: *"And the Quran is a proof for you or against you"* (Muslim). This means that if you seek to draw closer to Allah by believing and following its commands it will be a proof in your favour. However if you neglect its words and do not fulfil the obligations towards the Quran it will be a witness against you.

2. The Quran will Intercede for Us on the Day of Judgement

See Chapter 10 on Well-being in the Life after Death.

3. The Quran Raises One's Status in this Life

This has been stated by the Messenger of Allah ﷺ: *"Verily, Allah raises the status of people with this book and by it he humbles others"* (Muslim 817).

4. Recitation of the Quran is highly rewarded by Allah

We learn from the Hadith that *"Whoever reads a letter from the Book of Allah, he will have a reward, and this reward will be multiplied by ten. I am not saying that 'Alif, Lam, Meem' (a combination of letters frequently mentioned in the Holy Quran) is a letter, rather I am saying that 'Alif' is a letter, 'Lam' is a letter and 'Meem' is a letter"* (At-Tirmidhi).

5. The People of the Quran are among the best of People

'Uthman said that the Prophet ﷺ said: *"The best of you are those who learn the Quran and teach it to others"* (Al-Bukhari).

6. The Reciters of the Quran Will Be in the Company of the Noble and Obedient Angels

Aa'ishah related that the Prophet ﷺ said: *"Indeed the one who recites the Quran beautifully, smoothly, and precisely, will be in the company of the noble and obedient angels. As for the one who recites with difficulty, stammering or stumbling through its verses, then he will have twice that reward"* (Al-Bukhari and Muslim).

7. The Quran Leads us to Paradise

We are told that "Indeed the Quran guides to that which is most suitable and gives good tidings to the believers who do righteous deeds that they will have a great reward" [Quran: 17:9].

8. The level a person reaches in Paradise is Determined by the Amount of Quran He Memorised in this Life

Abdullah bin 'Amr bin Al-'Aas heard the Prophet ﷺ saying: *"It will be said to the companion of the Quran: 'Read and elevate (through the levels of Paradise) and beautify your voice as you did when you were in the worldly life! For verily, your position in Paradise will be at the last verse you recite'"* (Abu Dawood and At-Tirmithi).

DUA

We all face trials and difficulties in life. It is during these times that we need to turn to Allah for help. Dua or invocation to Allah is the beautiful and blessed time we have in solitude with Allah when we beg for His forgiveness and for all the things we need from Him, as well as asking Him to alleviate our troubles. It is an opportunity for us to pour out our hearts to Him. Dua relieves distress, brings us closer to Allah and can change our Qadr. Muhammad ﷺ said *"Nothing can change the Divine decree except Dua"* (Ahmad 5/677; Ibn Maajah 90; al Tirmidhi, 139).

We should never underestimate the power of Dua. If we approach Allah with faith and humility, He will surely help us. We must remember that Allah has promised to respond to our Duas. In the Glorious Quran He states: **"And when My servants ask you, [O Muhammad], concerning Me - indeed I am near. I respond to the invocation of the supplicant when he calls upon Me. So let them respond to Me [by obedience] and believe in Me that they may be [rightly] guided"** (2:186).

However if we do not see an immediate result from our Duas we must not despair. Many think the response can only be one outcome, i.e. our wish being granted for example being given a new job, house or marriage. In fact Allah has supreme knowledge of our affairs and our supplication will be answered in a way and at a time that Allah knows to be best for us. Our Duas are never wasted: It was narrated from Abu Sa'id that the Prophet ﷺ said: *"There is no Muslim who does not offer any Dua in which there is no sin or severing of family ties but Allah will give him one of three things in return: either He will answer his Dua sooner, or he will store it up for him in the Hereafter, or He will divert an equivalent evil away from him because of it"* (Ahmad: 10749).

REPENTANCE (TAUBAH)

We know that our Iman (faith) fluctuates, sometimes being strong and at other times weak. On top of that we are continuously targeted with the whisperings and distractions of Shaytan. This makes us vulnerable to making mistakes and falling into sin. Therefore we should turn to Allah in sincere repentance and approach Him with hope in His mercy and forgiveness, of which we are assured in the Quran: "But whoever repents after

Allah is "Ghafur ur-Raheem" (extremely merciful and forgiving), we are reminded of this 72 times in the Quran. He gives us ample opportunities up until the end of our lives to make Taubah (repent) and follow the path of righteousness.

his wrongdoing and reforms, indeed Allah will turn to him in forgiveness. Indeed, Allah is Forgiving and Merciful" (5:39).

True repentance is not merely in words spoken by the tongue. Rather it has to include leaving the sin, regretting the action and firmly resolving not to return to it.

The Benefits of seeking Forgiveness as promised in the Quran

- Perpetual forgiveness of sins (Surah Nuh:10)
- Provision of gardens and rivers (Surah Nuh:12)
- Continuous rain showers (Surah Nuh:11)
- Increase in wealth and children (Surah Nuh:12)
- Increase in strength (Surah Hud:52)
- Enjoyment of good provision (Surah Hud:3)
- Relief from affliction and punishment (Surah Al-Anfal:33)
- Allah loves those who repent (Surah Baqarah:222)

The Dua below is known as the Sayyid al-Istighfar and is the most superior way of asking for forgiveness from Allah. Muhammad ﷺ was reported to have said: *"If someone recites it during the day with firm faith in it, and dies on the same day before the evening, he will be from the people of Paradise; and if somebody recites it at night with firm faith in it, and dies before the morning, he will be from the people of Paradise:*

اللهم أنت ربي لا إله إلّا أنت خلقتني وأنا عبدك، وأنا على عهدك ووعدك ما استطعت، أعوذ بك من شر ما صنعت، أبوء لك بنعمتك علي، وأبوء بذنبي فاغفر لي فإنّه لا يغفر الذنوب إلّا أنت

Allahumma anta Rabbi la ilaha illa anta. Anta khalaqtani wa ana abduka, wa ana 'ala ahdika wa wa'dika mastata'tu, A'udhu bika min sharri ma sana'tu, abu'u laka bini'matika 'alaiya, wa abu laka bidhanbi faghfirli, innahu la yaghfiru adhdhunuba illa anta. (O Allah! You are my Lord! None has the right to be worshipped but You. You created me and I am Your slave, and I am faithful to my covenant and my promise as much as I can. I seek refuge with You from all the evil I have done. I acknowledge before You all the blessings You have bestowed upon me, and I confess to You all my sins. So I entreat You to forgive my sins, for nobody can forgive sins except You)" (Al-Bukhari 8, 75 #318).

SALAH

Salah or praying five times a day is one of the pillars of Islam and is an act of worship filled with praise and glorification of Allah. It is the first deed we will be asked about on the Day of Judgment: The Prophet ﷺ said: *"The first thing for which a person will be brought to account on the Day of*  *Resurrection will be his prayer. If it is sound, he will be successful, and if it is lacking in any way, he will be doomed. If his obligatory prayers are lacking, the Lord will say: 'Look and see whether My slave has any voluntary prayers which may be used to make up what is lacking in his obligatory prayers.' Then all his deeds will be examined and dealt with in the same way"* (Al-Tirmidhi: 413).

It is one of the great gifts from Allah Almighty that He has enjoined Salah upon believers, thereby providing us with a constant means to strengthen our faith and belief by remembering Him throughout the day. We offer Salah to be close to Allah and to gain His favour.

How Salah improves our spiritual wellbeing

1. Salah is a beautiful act of worship which deepens our connection to Allah, especially when performed five times a day. The act of bowing and prostrating causes us to become humble and submissive before our Lord as well as enabling us to express our gratitude to Him. The Prophet ﷺ said: *"Prayer is the best thing to be occupied with, so perform as much of it as you can"* (Ahmad).

2. It provides inner peace and serenity to the worshipper; this is portrayed in Muhammad's ﷺ eagerness to perform Salah when he called upon Bilal: *"O Bilal! Call the Iqamah in order for our hearts to relax"* (Ahmad and Abu Dawud).

3. Salah helps us to develop patience and gives us the spiritual strength to take us through life's endeavours.

4. Salah protects us from Shaytan and restrains the believer from indecent and sinful deeds. By standing before Allah we are provided with a regular means of repentance and are purified of our sins. Abu Huraira reported: The Messenger of Allah ﷺ said, *"If there was a river at the door of anyone of you and he took a bath in it five times a day, would you notice any dirt on him?" The companions said, "Not a trace of dirt would be left." The Prophet said, "That is the parable of the five prayers by which*

Allah removes sins" (Al-Bukhari: 505, and Muslim: 667).

5. Praying repeatedly throughout the day and interrupting our daily activities to remember Allah increases our devotion to Him and reminds us that our purpose in life is to worship Him. It also helps us to detach from the Dunya (world).

6. To prevent distracting thoughts and develop focus (khushoo) in Salah, Prophet Muhammad ﷺ recommended that we seek refuge in Allah from Shaytan: 'Uthman ibn Abi'l-'Aas, went to the Prophet ﷺ and said: *"O Messenger of Allah, the Shaytan interferes between me and my prayer and my recitation, and he makes me confused." The Messenger of Allah ﷺ said: "That is a devil called Khanzab. If you feel that, then seek refuge with Allah from him and spit dryly to your left three times." 'Uthman said: "I did that and Allah took him away from me"* (Muslim: 2203).

7. Salah is a means of support and assistance in times of distress and grief. The Prophet ﷺ always used to turn to prayer whenever he was distressed, and we should follow his example.

> The Tahajjud prayer performed in the last third of the night is a special opportunity for us to have our difficulties alleviated and our prayers answered as Allah descends to the lowest heaven to respond to our Duas.

8. Last but not least performing Salah is an act of obedience to Allah and is highly rewarded by Him. In the Holy Quran we are assured that "Those who believe and do deeds of righteousness, and establish regular prayers and regular charity — they will have their reward with their Lord. On them shall be no fear, nor shall they grieve" (2:277).

FASTING

Ramadan is the sacred month in which we come close to our Creator by fasting and performing additional prayers and good deeds in order to please Him. Families and communities are united in the evenings as we share food to break our fasts together and then pray in congregation at the masjid, everyone  standing equal in the sight of Allah. Fasting teaches self-restraint and is good for the mind, body and spirit.

Unlike prayers, charity and pilgrimage fasting is a secret act of worship known only to Allah and the person who is fasting. It increases piety and sincerity in the person as fasting is done purely for the sake of Allah. The superiority of fasting over other acts of worship is illustrated in the Hadith Qudsi in which Allah says: *"Every good action is rewarded by ten times its kind, up to seven hundred times, except fasting, which is for Me, and I reward it"* (Sahih Bukhari: 31/118). Thus the magnitude of the reward gained through fasting is known only to Allah.

Fasting teaches discipline and self- control. We learn to control our appetite and desires, gratification which is normally permissible but forbidden during fasting. This trains us to be able to resist the things which are completely forbidden (haram) when we are not in a state of fasting. As fasting strengthens our Iman we develop a consciousness of Allah that makes it much easier to carry out other acts of obedience to Allah. Hence fasting in Ramadan is often coupled with Muslims making generous donations of charity and Zakat. In addition when we experience the pangs of hunger we are able to develop empathy for the poor and destitute and feel gratitude towards Allah for all he has blessed us with.

Physical and mental benefits of fasting
See Chapter 1 on Healthy Bodies.

DHIKR

Dhikr is when we praise and glorify Allah by repeating short phrases or prayers in the mind, quietly or aloud. It is a vital act of Ibadah in our beautiful religion and also contributes to our wellbeing, for we are told in the Quran: *"Verily in the Remembrance of Allah do hearts find rest"* (13:28).

Some benefits of Dhikr
1. It is one of the easiest forms of worship yet is still highly rewarded by Allah. Dhikr is the unique type of worship that can be practised while sitting, standing, lying or indeed while engaged in most of our day-to-day activities.
2. Through Dhikr a believer is relieved of troubles, worries and fears, and is blessed with Sakinah (peace and tranquillity). He can repent for his sins, and acquire protection from the devils who are around him. It makes him remember that every minute of our life in this

world is precious if we want to earn the treasures of the next life.

3. It leads to success as mentioned in the Quran: *"And remember Allah much, that you may be successful"* (62:10).

4. Dhikr can be a substitute for voluntary acts of worship which some people may not be in a position to accomplish. It is related in one Hadith that the poor people once complained to the Messenger of Allah ﷺ of the higher reward available to the rich because of their wealth: The companions said *"These rich men offer prayers and fast just as we do, but they excel us by performing Umrah and Hajj, and by taking part in Jihad on account of their wealth."* The Messenger ﷺ replied: *"Should I tell you something, so that none except one who practices it can excel you."* He then advised them to recite:

سبحان الله - الحمد لله - الله اكبر

'Subhanallah, Alhamdulilah, Allahu Akbar.'"

5. Dhikr strengthens the body and mind making us more productive and successful. Once Fatimah complained to her father, the Messenger of Allah ﷺ, of excessive fatigue due to grinding wheat and other domestic chores. She asked whether a servant could be arranged for her. The Messenger ﷺ advised her to recite "Subhanallah" and "Alhamdulillah" each 33 times and "Allahhu Akbar" 34 times.

You can purchase or download a booklet of Adhkar (Prayers) e.g. *Hisnul Muslim* or *The Fortress of a Muslim*. Recite from it whenever you are free throughout the day, particularly the morning and evening Adhkar which can be recited on your way to school, university or work. In a few weeks, you'll find that you've already memorized those Adhkar and can recite them easily throughout the day.

The Prophet ﷺ further said to her: *"The recitation of these Kalimas is better for you than a servant"* (Abu Dawud).

6. Dhikr provides protection against Hell-fire and the Angels pray for the forgiveness of those who are engaged in Dhikr.

7. Those who remember Allah will earn His pleasure and receive His countless and everlasting mercy, favours and bounties. To gain the love of Allah one should engage in abundant Dhikr for Allah promises us in the Quran "Remember me, and I will remember you" (2:152).

8. It increases our Tawakul or reliance on Allah. By doing Dhikr we are reminded that Almighty Allah is our sole Provider who takes care of all our needs.

The following are some Adhkar that can easily be incorporated into our daily lives:

سُبْحَانَ اللّهِ، والْحَمْدُللّهِ، وَلاِلهَ إلا اللّهُ، وَاللّهُ اَكْبَرُ

- "SubhanAllah, walHamdulilah, wa La illaha ilAllahu, wa Allahu Akbar" (Glory be to Allah, All Praise is for Allah, There is No God but Allah, Allah is the Greatest). The above are mentioned as the four most beloved words to Allah. It does not matter with which one of them is begun (Muslim: 3/1685).

سُبْحَانَ اللّهِ

- "SubhanAllah (Glory be to Allah)." Whoever recites this 100 times, 1000 good deeds are recorded for him or 1000 bad deeds are wiped away (Muslim; 4/2073).

- Abu Hurairah reported: The Messenger of Allah ﷺ said, *"He who recites after every prayer: 'Subhan Allah' (Allah is free from imperfection) 33 times; 'Alhamdu lillah' (praise be to Allah) 33 times; 'Allahu Akbar' (Allah is Greatest) 33 times; and completes the hundred with:*

لا اله إلا وحده لا شريك له له الملك و له الحمد و هو على كل شيء قدير

'La ilaha illallahu, wahdahu la sharika lahu, lahul-mulku wa lahul-hamdu, wa Huwa `ala kulli shay'in Qadir' (there is no true god except Allah. He is One and He has no partner with Him. His is the sovereignty and His is the praise, and He is Omnipotent), will have all his sins pardoned even if they may be as large as the foam on the surface of the sea" (Muslim).

● If on any day a person repeats the following words 100 times:

لا اله إلا وحده لا شريك له له الملك و له الحمد و هو على كل شيء قدير

"There is none worthy of worship except Allah, the One. There is no partner with Him; His is the kingdom, and for Him is all praise, and He has power over everything." He is rewarded as much as for freeing 10 slaves, and in addition 100 virtues are written in his account and 100 sins are forgiven. He remains protected against the devil throughout the day, and none is considered as having acted better than him except one who has recited the same words more often than he did (Al-Bukhari and Sahih Muslim).

● The Prophet ﷺ said, *"There are two expressions which are very easy for the tongue to say, but they are very heavy in the balance and are very dear to The Beneficent (Allah), and they are:*

سبحان الله وبحمده سبحان الله العظيم

'SubhanAllahi wa bihamdihi' and 'SubhanAllahi al-`Azim'" (Al-Bukhari and Muslim) .

● Muhammad ﷺ said: *"Whoever sends blessings upon me once, Allah will send blessings upon him tenfold and will erase from him 10 misdeeds and raise him 10 degrees in status"* (An-Nasa'i: 1297).

- Reciting Surah al-Ikhlas is equivalent to one-third of the Quran as stated by the Messenger of Allah ﷺ: *"By the One in Whose hand is my soul, it is equivalent to one-third of the Quran"* (Al-Bukhari).

- Abu Musa al-Ash'ari reported that Allah's Messenger ﷺ said to him: *"Should I not direct you to the words from the treasures of Paradise; or he said: Like a treasure from the treasures of Paradise?" I said: "Of course, do so." Thereupon he said:*

  لا حَوْلَ وَلا قُوَّةَ إلا بِالله

  "There is no might and no power but that of Allah." (Al-Bukhari and Muslim)

- It was narrated from Juwayriyyah that the Prophet ﷺ left her house one morning when he prayed Fajr, and she was in her prayer-place, then he came back after the forenoon had come, and she was still sitting there. *He said: "Are you still as you were when I left you?" She said: "Yes." The Prophet ﷺ said: "After I left you I said four words three times, which if they were weighed against what you have said today, they would outweigh it:*

  سُبْحـانَ اللهِ وَبِحَمْدِهِ عَدَدَ خَلْقِه ، وَرِضا نَفْسِه ، وَزِنَةَ عَـرْشِـه ، وَمِـداد كَلِمـاتِه

  'Subhaan Allah wa bi hamdih, 'adada khalqihi, wa ridaa nafsihi, wazinata 'arshihi, wa midaada kalimaatihi' (Glory and praise be to Allah, as much as the number of His creation, as much as pleases Him, as much as the weight of His Throne and as much as the ink of His words)" (Muslim: 2726).

The beauty of Dhikr is that the words or short phrases that we recite are not only soothing to the heart and soul but also protect us, and are a means to gain abundant rewards from Allah. We are told in the Quran that "… the men and the women who remember Allah much with their hearts and tongues Allah has prepared for them forgiveness and a great reward (i.e. Paradise)" (33:35).

If we can develop the habit to do Dhikr regularly it will be of tremendous benefit to us. We should share with others the knowledge about the virtues of Dhikr so they can also receive blessings and rewards. May Allah enable us all to constantly remember Him; to keep our tongues moist with Dhikr and fill the record of our deeds with it. Ameen.

6. Purification of the Heart

Purification of the heart is vital for our health and wellbeing. Prophet Muhammad ﷺ is reported to have said *"Truly in the body there is a morsel of flesh which, if it be whole, all the body is whole and which, if it be diseased, all of it is diseased. Truly it is the heart"*

(Al-Bukhari and Muslim). This is why it is so important to recognise diseases of the heart (Qalb), ask Allah for assistance and then constantly work to purify the condition of our hearts. Our success in the Hereafter depends on this.

There are many diseases that can afflict the heart. However among them are a few we should be particularly cautious of because of the damage they do to the heart and because they can produce additional vices like backbiting, greed and selfishness. Envy, takabbur (pride) and holding grudges are examples of such diseases.

ENVY (HASAD)

Qualities in others such as academic achievement, prestige and wealth can create envy or Hasad. Prophet Muhammad ﷺ warned us against envy and its serious consequences by saying *"Beware, save yourselves from Hasad. Verily Hasad devours virtuous deeds as fire devours wood"* (Abu Dawud). When feeling jealous of

someone we often wonder what he has done to deserve such privileges. But it is not for us to question why Allah has blessed some people with more than others as we are reminded in the Quran that *"Allah Provides sustenance to whom He pleases without measure"* (3:37).

By harbouring jealousy in our heart, we allow ill feelings to fester including hatred towards the person of whom we are jealous. This can result in us casting the evil eye on the person which may end up harming him.

How do we protect the person who is the target of our jealousy against the Evil Eye?

We need to make Dua for the blessing of Allah upon that person by saying

اللهم بارك عليه

"Allahumma baarik `alaih" (O Allah send your blessings upon him). We must also remember that the Messenger of Allah ﷺ has instructed us that *"If one of you looks at a person who is better than him in wealth and body, let him look at the people beneath him"* (Muslim). By considering those who have less we automatically start to see all the blessings Allah has bestowed upon us.

Though it will not come naturally we should try to generate good feelings towards the person we envy, speak well of him to others and remind ourselves that whatever he has are Allah's favours on him.

ARROGANCE (TAKABBUR)

Arrogance or Takabbur is a characteristic in which one feels superior to others e.g. with regards to wealth, knowledge, beauty, lineage, etc. The first one who showed arrogance towards Allah and His creation was the accursed Iblis (Shaytan) when Allah commanded him to prostrate to Adam ﷺ. He refused by saying: *"I am better than him (Adam). You created me from fire, and Him You created from clay"* (Quran 7:12). Shaytan's pride brought about his downfall and caused him to be dismissed from divine presence as an unbeliever.

Arrogance may be the cause of a person being deprived of Jannah: it was narrated by Abdullah ibn Masud that the Prophet ﷺ said *"No one who has an atom's weight of pride in his heart will enter paradise"* (Muslim: 164).

How can we rid ourselves of Takabbur?

- We should remember that nothing we have belongs to us. Our bodies, clothes, homes, cars and possessions are all owned by Allah and can be taken away from us at any time. So how can we feel proud of what we have?

- We have to remind ourselves of our end, that when we die we are going to end up in the earth, taking nothing with us except our good deeds.
- The act of glorifying Allah and asking for our sins to be forgiven makes us humble and removes arrogance from our hearts.
- Studying the life of our beloved Prophet ﷺ shows us how humble he was. There is a famous Hadith by Umar ibn Al-Khattab ؓ. He mentions that he entered the mosque in Medina where the Prophet ﷺ was lying down in his small dwelling. The simplicity of his home with a few meagre possessions moved Umar to tears. *The Prophet ﷺ asked "Ibn Khattab, what makes you weep?" Umar answered "Messenger of Allah, why should I not shed tears? This mat [which the Prophet ﷺ was lying on] has left its marks on your sides and I do not see in your store room [except these few things] that I have seen. Caesar and Closroes are leading their lives in plenty whereas you are Allah's Messenger, His chosen one, and that is your store!" The Prophet ﷺ said "Ibn Khattab, aren't you satisfied that for us is the prosperity of the hereafter and for them the prosperity of this world?"* (Sahih Muslim 1479) Muhammad ﷺ and his household remained indifferent to building or possessing any more than was necessary. He chose to lead a modest life despite having undisputed leadership and the power to live in luxury.

BEARING GRUDGES

Bearing a grudge against someone is a feeling of resentment which is so deep seated that a person is unable to forgive or forget someone else's mistakes or ill treatment of them. Sometimes, sadly it may just be a misunderstanding which no one has had the courage or the will to sort out. At other times someone may not even be aware that they have done something wrong, or that a person is holding a grudge against them.

Our beloved Prophet ﷺ would be quick to forgive as he knew that treating his enemies well would ultimately lead to the spread of Islam. When he was taunted and stoned in the city of Taif Allah sent an angel at the Prophet's disposal to crush the people of Taif. But the Prophet ﷺ overlooked what they had done and chose to forgive and forget. He even made Dua for the people of Taif and their children to become Muslim. Allah answered his prayers and to this day Taif remains a thriving city of Islam.

> People who bear grudges spend their lives carrying around a heavy burden of negativity and resentment. This is unhealthy both psychologically and spiritually.

We are often hurt by the people who are closest to us and this is when the pain is felt more acutely because it comes from a place we didn't expect. A notable example of forgiveness and compassion comes from Abu Bakr (As-Siddiq) ﷺ during the incident of slander against his beloved daughter A'ishah ﷺ. Abu Bakr had a cousin, Mistah Bin Uthathah whom he supported financially. When Abu Bakr discovered that Mistah was also involved in spreading false rumours about Aisha he vowed not to help Mistah anymore. Subsequently Surah Nur, verse 22 of the Quran was revealed. Allah the Exalted said: "Let them pardon and overlook. Would you not love for Allah to forgive you? Allah is Forgiving and Merciful." This resulted in Abu Bakr resuming his financial help to Mistah (Al-Bukhari). We should try to emanate these examples and earn the pleasure of Allah through forgiving others. Allah has described the believers as "those who avoid the major sins and immoralities, and when they are angry, forgive" (42:37). We should overlook people's shortcomings and seek reconciliation with those who have angered us. Forgiveness is not always easy but it is the only way to truly let go and have peace.

SOME METHODS TO ACHIEVE PURIFICATION OF THE HEART

Seek refuge in Allah and put your trust in Him
Repentance and sincere supplications (Dua). A frequent supplication of the Messenger of Allah ﷺ was:

يَا مُقَلِّبَ الْقُلُوبِ ثَبِّتْ قَلْبِى عَلَى دِينِكَ

"O, Turner of the hearts, turn our hearts to Your obedience" (Tirmidhi: 2140).

Do regular Dhikr (remembrance of Allah)
This nourishes the heart.

Befriend righteous people who influence you and guide you to acts of obedience to Allah

The righteous friend is one who will:

- Give you sincere advice: guide you to do good and forbid what is wrong.
- Will always be ready to help you. He will join you in times of difficulty as well as ease, and not remind you of any favours he does for you.
- Will not envy you and will rejoice when he sees the blessings Allah has given you.
- Will share beneficial knowledge with you and encourage you to participate in activities to gain Allah's pleasure.
- Will remind you of Allah and love you for the sake of Allah.

Practice Muhassabah (self-assessment)

We need to question ourselves about our nafs and our actions. By reviewing our weaknesses and shortcomings regularly we can ask for forgiveness from Allah and correct ourselves.

Praying to Allah to guide others and ease their difficulties

This removes ill feeling and hatred from our hearts and enables us to love others for the sake of Allah. It is of particular benefit to us to make Dua for others as any Dua that we make for our Muslim brothers or sisters will be granted to us too. This is confirmed by the Hadith: *"He who supplicates for his brother behind his back (in his absence), the angel commissioned (for carrying Dua to his Lord) says: 'Ameen, and it is for you also'"* (Muslim).

Remembering the Hereafter and the Day of Judgement

This makes us less attached to the world and helps us to view life as a journey. This also helps us to let go of past pain, anger and resentment as we realise life is too short to hold onto the past.

Sadaqah

When we donate from our wealth in charity this removes worldliness from our hearts and envy of what others have. Other acts of charity like showing kindness and helping people increase our empathy and understanding of others and help purify the heart. We are also able to appreciate all the blessings Allah has bestowed upon us.

The state of our hearts is what will benefit us because our actions will be judged by our intentions. We should cleanse our heart of all diseases and free it from the unnecessary burdens of the Dunya. Only then can we return to the Almighty with a Qalbin Salim (sound heart); "When the only one who will be saved is the one who comes before Allah with a heart devoted to Him" (26:88).

7. Healthy Relationships

 Healthy relationships are ones that bring out the best in us and they are essential for our health and wellbeing. We are able to connect with others through positive interactions and can rely on our loved ones for support, care and affection.

MARRIAGE

Marriage is strongly encouraged in Islam. It is an institution that forms the foundation of Islamic society and ensures continuation of the Ummah (Muslim community). It develops love and commitment between spouses and is the means by which relationships are recognised and sanctified so that desires can be fulfilled in a halal (permissible) way. Marriage leads to reproduction and the formation of a family through which one can find security, stability and peace of mind.

Love

We are reminded in the Quran that Allah bestows love between husband and wife: **"And of His signs is that He created for you from yourselves mates that you may find tranquillity in them; and He placed between you affection and mercy. Indeed in that are signs for a people who give thought"** (30:21).

A healthy marriage will include feelings of Compassion, a sense of care and concern from your spouse and knowing that they are there to support you. In a good relationship your spouse will be kind to you, will understand you and help you in difficult times. Loyalty is another important feature:

> All marriages have ups and downs but good communication can make it easier to resolve conflict and build a stronger and healthier relationship.

when your spouse is reliable and you feel confident that they will back you. There are many more elements to maintaining a healthy marriage. However the points below give a few tips on how to develop a good relationship with your spouse.

Tips for couples

- Focus on obligations, not rights. This makes it much easier to fulfil your duties towards each other. If you serve and look after one another for the sake of Allah you will feel content and He will put blessing into your marriage.
- Maintain some humour and light heartedness in your relationship. Life does not have to be serious all the time and laughter can strengthen the bond of marriage.

- Cultivate and refine good manners towards each other. Take each other's feelings into consideration when conversing or making decisions.
- Take time to dress well and smell pleasant.
- Ask Allah to strengthen and preserve the bond of marriage whenever you make Dua.
- Conflicts should be dealt with sensitively and early on, rather than being allowed to fester and emerge time and time again.
- Spouses should respect each other's differences and not try to control or change one another. Nobody appreciates being nagged or forced to change themselves to suit someone else.
- Keep each other's secrets safe and offer good advice and help when necessary.
- Don't criticise each other or use ridicule or sarcasm, especially in front of others. On the contrary praising each other especially in the company of family or friends will go a long way towards strengthening the marriage.

TIPS FOR WIVES

Be content in your husband's company. Listen to him and obey him for this is a gateway to Paradise - as narrated by Anas ibn Malik: *"Allah's Messenger ﷺ said, 'When a woman observes the five times of prayer, fasts during Ramadan, preserves her chastity and obeys her husband, she may enter by any of the gates of Paradise she wishes'"* (Al- Tirmidhi: 3254).

Good Housekeeping. Prepare his food on time. Every so often make his favourite dishes to please him. Keep the house clean and tidy- a clean house is important for the health and well-being of your entire family.

Give him some time to himself when he comes home from work. A woman sometimes assumes that if she asks her husband lots of questions about his day at work he will be prepared to listen to her. This doesn't always work. Men like to have some time alone to contemplate in front of the TV or their device. This helps them to unwind and sort out their problems

"Men are the protectors and maintainers of women"(Quran 4:34). A significant and beautiful feature of Islam is that it is a woman's right to be looked after from cradle to grave. Before marriage it is the duty of her father to financially support her. And after marriage it is her husband who needs to provide for her. Women may choose to work and help to support the family but they are under no obligation to do so. Financial responsibility is shouldered by the husband and a wife needs to respect him for performing this role. She should show gratitude and appreciation towards him. A man can be stressed out from a day at work but if his wife is happy with him he feels fulfilled. He thrives on successfully caring for and providing for his family.

An important aspect of the marriage is the physical relationship. For a man it is often more of a priority because it gives him reassurance that you are strong and connected as a couple. It is also an indication of a healthy marriage.

A man likes to take on a challenge. For example, doing a repair job or some DIY in the house. Don't doubt his ability to carry out a task or make a decision. Compliment him and thank him for what he does.

TIPS FOR HUSBANDS

Treat your wife with kindness. It was narrated from Ibn 'Abbas that the Prophet ﷺ said: *"The best of you is the one who is best to his wife, and I am the best of you to my wives"* (Ibn Majah: 1977).

In Surah Baqarah we are told: **"And they (women) have rights (over their husbands as regards living expenses) similar (to those of their husbands) over them (as regards obedience and respect) to what is reasonable, but men have a degree (of** responsibility) over them. And Allah is All-Mighty, All-Wise"** (2:228).

Thus a man's role is of leadership in relation to his family but this does not mean the husband's dictatorship over his wife. Islam emphasizes the importance of taking advice and mutual agreement when making decisions within the family.

There is truth in the saying "A woman's work is never done". She has to handle many different aspects of life. She needs to attend to her husband, raise the children, their education, tarbiyyah (Islamic training) and appointments, not to mention the myriad of chores around the house. She is stretched in all directions and her work is unpaid in monetary terms, and at times invisible. Therefore it is good that men acknowledge and appreciate how much their wives do, and help out with the children's upbringing, tarbiyyah and housework: *A'ishah, the wife of the Prophet Muhammad ﷺ as asked, "What did the Prophet used to do in his house?" She replied, "He used to keep himself busy serving his family and when it was the time for prayer he would go for it"* (Al-Bukhari).

Look at her qualities rather than her faults. A man is often quick to notice his wife's shortcomings or ways in which she annoys him. Why not focus on the positive aspects of her nature? The importance of this has been

> Indeed our Prophet Muhammad ﷺ is the best among men and when he himself looked after his family and home why shouldn't husbands follow his example?

emphasised in the Quran: "But consort with them in kindness, for if you hate them it may happen that you hate a thing wherein God has placed much good" (4:19).

COMMUNICATION

It is vital to communicate clearly with each other to avoid misunderstandings that can lead to hurt or anger. Effective communication also includes listening to your spouse and trying to understand their feelings and needs.

Women need emotional connection as well as physical. They

thrive when they feel loved. The marriage will be strengthened if a husband listens to his wife with care and attention. She may not always be looking for solutions; sometimes women just feel overwhelmed and want to off load whatever is on their mind. It is important to be reassuring and sympathetic.

Husbands, share your difficulties and worries with your wife as well as your ambitions and successes; after all marriage is about support and companionship. Keep in touch through text or phone calls when you have time at work. Women  like to talk and share- if this need is fulfilled through quality and thoughtful conversations this will draw you closer as a couple and enhance the physical relationship too.

HEALTHY RELATIONSHIPS WITH CHILDREN

Our children are a great blessing from Allah
They are also an Amanah or Trust from Him to us. Therefore it is our duty to educate, train and protect them so that with the help of Allah they grow into righteous and responsible Muslims. For this it is important for us as parents to provide the right Islamic environment for our children to thrive. (Please also refer to my book *A Guide to Muslim Parenting*.)

Children should be treated with mercy and kindness

Our beloved Prophet ﷺ is reported to have said: *"He who does not show mercy to others, will not be shown mercy"* (Al-Bukhari and Muslim). As well as teaching children rituals of Islam like performing Salah and recitation of the Quran they should also be taught the Adab and Akhlaq (manners) of interacting with others particularly their parents, elders and visitors. This will lead to good relationships especially if children are encouraged to follow the practices of the Messenger of Allah ﷺ who was the best in manners.

Talk to your children and take their choices and opinions into consideration.

Children need to feel supported. It is important to create an atmosphere of approval and appreciation in the household so that everyone is valued. This boosts self-esteem and productivity of family members and enhances the wellbeing of the household.

Families should try to perform Salah (prayers) together and have family circles for studying the Quran and developing knowledge of Islam. As well as uniting the family this will bring reward and blessing to the home Insha Allah.

Spend time with your children

As well as playing with them it is a good idea to do some work together, e.g. baking or setting the table. Even a spot of DIY. This builds relationships and improves confidence and competence in children.

As far as possible have mealtimes together

This is encouraged in the Sunnah as it brings blessings to Muslims. The Messenger of Allah ﷺ said *"Eat together and mention the Name of Allah over your food. It will be blessed for you"* (Abu Dawud). Eating together helps family members maintain relationships and feel a sense of belonging. Meals prepared at home will tend to be more healthy and the time spent together can bring about an air of warmth, comfort and happiness. Family mealtimes are also an opportunity for children to learn from table talk and express their own ideas as well as catching up with everyone.

Children should be told and shown that they are loved

Hugs and kisses release oxytocin (the love hormone). This naturally occurring hormone in our bodies is incredibly good for our health. It helps children's bodies to grow and contributes to healthy brain development. Hugging a child can calm him during a temper tantrum and improves mood generally.

In fact hugging and kissing is good for everyone in the family. Oxytocin gives pain relief and boosts the immune system by increasing hormones that fight infection. It also helps to reduce levels of stress and anxiety and deepens relationships by creating love, warmth and bonding.

HEALTHY RELATIONSHIPS WITH PARENTS

Parenting can be challenging especially in modern times yet

parents remain selfless and sacrificial, showing unconditional love in raising their children. Fathers work hard for the best part of their lives to provide food, clothing, protection and comfort for their families. Mothers fulfil their roles by bearing children, then nursing and looking after them, often well into adulthood. So it is no wonder that after Allah our parents deserve our obedience and thanks for all the favours they do for us.

When children are young they are eager for interaction and spending time with parents. But as the years go by the situation reverses and parents start to yearn for the attention of their children. As parents age they become more set in their ways. Illnesses and weakness can lead to lack of energy, heightened sensitivity and dependence on children. We need to give them our time and treat them with gentleness and compassion to improve their wellbeing. Even the choice of words and tone of our voice to be used with parents is addressed in the Noble Quran: "And your Lord has decreed that you not worship except Him, and to parents, good treatment. Whether one or both of them reach old age [while] with you, say not to them [so much as] 'Uff,' and do not repel them but speak to them a noble word. And out of kindness, lower to them the wing of humility and say 'My Lord! Bestow on them Your Mercy even as they cherished me in childhood'" (17: 23-24).

Mothers in particular hold a high position in Islam

Their importance lies in the responsibilities placed upon them and the hardships they suffer during pregnancy, childbirth and nurturing their young. The precedence of mothers is confirmed by the Hadith when a man asked *"O Messenger of Allah! Who from amongst mankind warrants the best companionship from me?" He replied: "Your mother." The man asked: "Then who?" So he replied: "Your mother." The man then asked: "Then who?" The Prophet replied again: "Your mother." The man then asked: "Then who?" So he replied: "Then your father"* (Al-Bukhari: 5971 and Muslim: 7/2).

Mistreatment of parents cannot be taken lightly

It is a major sin, second only to ascribing partners with Allah. The Prophet ﷺ is reported to have said *"Shall I not inform you about the three major sins?"* Those who were present replied, *"Yes, O Messenger of Allah."* He said *"Associating partners with Allah and disobedience to parents,"* and sitting up from the reclining position, he continued, *"and telling lies and false testimony; beware of it"* (Al-Bukhari and Muslim).

On the other hand good treatment of parents rewards us both in this life and in the hereafter. Give them a smile, a hug or a gift to reassure them of your love. If parents are happy we will also be happy as the blessings of our parents leads to our success and wellbeing in life.

We increase our good deeds and the pleasure of Allah by treating our parents well and making Dua for them. Our parents wish nothing but good for us. They constantly pray for our success and happiness, similarly we should also get into the habit of making Dua for their health and wellbeing, and thank Allah for them. Our supplications for Allah to reward them, forgive them and have mercy on them will continue to benefit them (and us) even after they have departed from this world.

For example this is the prayer of Prophet Ibrahim ﷺ which can be made for our parents and for all Muslims.

رَبَّنَا اغْفِرْ لِي وَلِوَالِدَيَّ وَلِلْمُؤْمِنِينَ يَوْمَ يَقُومُ الْحِسَابِ

Rabbanaa ighfir lee waliwaalidayya walilmu'mineena yawma yaqoomul-hisaab (Our Lord! Forgive me and my parents and the believers on the Day when the account will be established) (14:41).

8. The Wellbeing of Others

Altruism, which is concern for the welfare of others not only benefits society in general but makes us feel better too. One of the best ways to feel personal happiness is by bringing joy to others. Happy people tend to be more sociable and caring of others. But it also works the other way round, i.e. helping other people is known to boost your own happiness. Studies have even found that people get more happiness from spending money on others than using it on themselves. Who has not experienced the joy of giving someone a gift? Or the pleasure of having guests round for dinner? It does not always have to involve spending money; giving can also be your time, energy or loving kindness; in short our lives are richer when we share.

Experiments show evidence that altruism is hardwired in the brain — and it is good for our wellbeing. It reduces stress and improves our health. As Islam teaches values that are intrinsic to human nature it is no wonder that we are constantly encouraged to help and to give to others. Abu Hurairah ﷺ reported: The Messenger of Allah ﷺ said, *"Whoever relieves a believer's distress of the distressful aspects of this world, Allah will rescue him from a difficulty of the difficulties of the Hereafter"* (Muslim).

> Selfless and compassionate acts can stimulate the brain to release endorphins which not only contribute to pleasure but are natural painkillers too. Helping others may lead to a life that is not only happier but more meaningful and productive too.

There are key questions we need to ask to help us discover what kind of Muslims we are and what sort of impression we leave: How significant are you to others? Is your presence felt? And will your absence be noticed? Who will cry when you die? What will you be remembered for long after you are gone?

Our personal acts of worship are valuable: visiting the masjid, fasting, performing Umrah and attending Islamic functions are all good but they are far from sufficient if they do not make us into better people. The following are questions that help us to assess how other people see us:

- Are you the one people turn to when they have a problem?
- When people need advice do they come to you because of your wisdom?
- When people have a dispute do they come to you because of your sense of justice?
- If they are hurt - perhaps they are grieving or going through a divorce - would they come to you for comfort?

Crowded city lives have made us feel more disconnected and less responsible for other people and therefore less willing to help them. We seem to be doing ordinary things mostly for the betterment of ourselves and our families. But we are falling short of looking after the community. Islam teaches us to provide service to humanity as exemplified by our beloved Prophet ﷺ who would often help others even if it meant that he had to sacrifice something. It is time we reached out and provided some benefit to others by small extraordinary deeds.

WHAT CAN WE DO FOR OTHERS?

- Visit a sick person regardless of their religion or race.
- Give someone a gift.
- Help someone elderly in the community by doing their shopping or housework or simply giving them some company.
- Mobilise people to assist others in times of crisis. Muslims were prompt to volunteer their help during the Grenfell Fire Disaster in London (2017) and the floods in Houston (2017).
- Organise events where people can learn something beneficial, e.g. self-development and health awareness.
- Volunteer to help at events eg Islamic functions/charity events at the Masjid or local community centre.
- Share your knowledge and wisdom through giving lectures or talks.
- Put a smile on someone's face by praising or complimenting them.
- Be a ray of sunshine for people if you are blessed with a positive

nature and optimism.
- Talk to the shy person at the office or school.
- Volunteer to mentor teenagers.
- Give extra lessons to someone who is not doing too well academically. Join hands to sponsor someone to further their education.
- Give someone a good reference when they apply for a job.

For the quieter ones amongst us:
- Help people silently by donating money for planting a tree or digging a well. Or set up a standing order with a chosen charity to donate money regularly.
- Write a book.
- Use social media to benefit others by sharing useful information and Islamic knowledge.
- Forward videos that are inspirational and highlight positives in our people.

The list goes on. Remember that nothing is too small- even a smile is charity. The important thing is to be consistent in helping others because A'ishah ﷺ reported that the Messenger of Allah ﷺ said: *"The deeds most loved by Allah (are those) done regularly, even if they are small"* (Al-Bukhari and Muslim).

SADAQAH

As Islam teaches us to show utmost respect and consideration for others we are encouraged to give Sadaqah (charity). As well as donating money, Sadaqah includes a wide range of other charitable acts. These are outlined in a beautiful hadith narrated by Abu Hurairah who said that *"the Messenger of Allah ﷺ said: "Every small bone of everyone has upon it a charitable act for everyday upon which the sun rises. Bringing about justice between two is an act of charity. Helping a man get on his mount, lifting him onto it or helping him put his belongings onto it, is a charitable act. A good word is a charitable act. Every step you take toward the prayer is a charitable act. And removing a harmful thing from the path is a charitable act"* (Al-Bukhari and Muslim). Islam emphasises goodness which is an innate part of human nature. Being a Muslim is a combination of being good

> Giving charity and performing other charitable acts not only contribute to the wellbeing of the individual but also promote wider benefits in society such as humanity, brotherhood and social equality.

and doing good. Our focus should be on touching lives and finding opportunities to provide benefit to others.

LOVING YOUR BROTHER FOR THE SAKE OF ALLAH

Islam also promotes meeting each other for no other purpose than to promote love and brotherhood: Abu Hurairah reported that the Prophet ﷺ said: *"A man set out to visit a brother (in Islam) in another town and Allah sent an angel on his way. When the man met the angel, the latter asked him, 'Where do you intend to go?' He said, 'I intend to visit my brother in this town.' The angel said, 'Have you done any favour to him?' He said, 'No, I have no desire except to visit him because I love him for the sake of Allah, the Exalted, and Glorious.' Thereupon the angel said, 'I am a messenger to you from Allah (to inform you) that Allah loves you as you love him (for His sake)'"* (Sahih Muslim). This Hadith points out the great merit of visiting Muslims for the sake of Allah and the value of Brotherhood in Islam.

THE ABUNDANT REWARD OF VISITING THE SICK

Ali said "I heard the Messenger of Allah ﷺ say: *"There is no Muslim who visits a (sick) Muslim early in the morning but seventy thousand angels send blessings upon him until evening comes, and if he visits him in the evening, seventy thousand angels send blessings upon him until morning comes, and he will have a garden in Paradise"* (Classed as Sahih by al-Albani in Sahih al-Tirmidhi).

We pray that we are able to perform good deeds purely for the sake of Allah, that they are accepted by Him and that whatever we do serves as a witness for us in the life to come. Ameen.

9. Wellbeing at Home

Islam promotes moderation and discourages extravagance. It emphasises that we should fulfil our needs adequately without wasting resources. Much of the teaching of Islam including the life of our beloved Prophet ﷺ illustrates the virtue of living a simple and minimalistic life. Minimalism means living with less. Adopting this approach helps us to let go of life's excesses in order to focus on what is really important. Unsurprisingly it is becoming popular amongst Muslims and non-Muslims.

ADVANTAGES OF MINIMALISM

- It frees up our mind. The more material possessions we have the more we have to worry about their cleaning, maintenance, protection, update and repair. Clearing our homes has a massive impact on our mental clarity and peace of mind.
- It helps us to reclaim our precious time. Allah says in the Holy Quran **"By time, Indeed mankind is in loss"** (103:1-2). When the mind is free we are able to contemplate and we can devote more

of our time and energy into fulfilling our obligations and doing meaningful things to attain the pleasure of Allah.

- A minimalist lifestyle enables us to have more rest and take better care of ourselves and our families
- A minimalist home is significantly less stressful. It is also much easier to clean and maintain.
- It reduces waste and extravagance which is discouraged in the Holy Quran "Children of Adam! Wear your beautiful apparel at every time and place of prayer and eat and drink. But do not be excessive-verily Allah does not love the wasteful" (7:31).
- We save money. Anyone buying less and using their time more constructively is bound to save a little extra cash. This can be used to support other causes.
- Life is temporary and all that we own will someday be dust. Minimalism helps us to remember death and focus on the real purpose of our life: to worship Allah.
- A minimalistic lifestyle gives us freedom from the pressure to compete or impress others. Prophet Muhammad ﷺ warned us about the danger of amassing wealth and competing for it. Amr ibn Awf ؓ reported: The Messenger of Allah ﷺ said, *"By Allah, it is not poverty I fear for you, but rather I fear you will be given the wealth of the world just as it was given to those before you. You will compete for it just as they competed for it and it will destroy you just as it destroyed them"* (Al-Bukhari: 2988 and Muslim: 2961).

There are many ways to incorporate elements of minimalism into your life. Amongst them are de-cluttering the home and living simply without getting caught up in consumerism. Reclaiming your time can also benefit your life significantly.

DE-CLUTTERING

De-cluttering put simply is the removal of unnecessary items from your home. How does de-cluttering improve your wellbeing? When you get rid of your stuff you are lightening your material burden and making room for something other than your possessions to take up your time and attention. The time released can be used to better purpose such as worship of Allah, recitation and memorisation of the Quran, acquiring beneficial knowledge and helping others.

> It is easier to carry out tasks in a clutter free home. People tend to feel like life is out of control when they have more things than they can manage. This can increase stress and adversely affect their wellbeing.

When you have unnecessary items in the home you are unable to use the space they occupy. You have to see them every day even if you don't use them, work around them or lift them every time you need to clean. This is a waste of time and energy.

De-cluttering is therapeutic. It not only cleanses your home but clears your mind. After de-cluttering the space in your rooms is clearer and there is a sense of order and calm around the home.

It improves efficiency: you have a better idea of where you have stored things in your home so you should be able to find them more easily and quickly.

De-cluttering can really improve the quality of life. It increases contentment, appreciation and gratitude as we are able to focus on all that Allah has blessed us with.

Tips to help you declutter

- Start de-cluttering now. There is no need to wait for the "right" time. Remember time will actually be released when you have to look after less stuff.
- De-cluttering does not imply throwing everything in the bin. A common technique used by people when they de-clutter is to divide items into four categories: discard, donate, keep, relocate.
- Discard things you have forgotten about – how important can they be if you haven't even missed them?
- When considering whether to discard something, ask yourself whether you have used it in the last six months, or a year? If you are not using something what is the point of keeping it?
- If you are still unsure of whether to discard an item store it away and check it after six months, or a year. Chances are you will have forgotten about it!
- At times you may feel guilty of discarding something; e.g. if it was expensive, or was a gift from someone. Perhaps you bought something but never used it. You need to remind yourself that the item is taking up valuable space in your home and mind.
- Discard something if you have it just for the sake of appearance; e.g. books which look worthy but no one actually reads. Send books to a charity shop or library. Islamic literature can be sent to a new masjid.
- Don't make the mistake of buying more storage units or containers. These will simply relocate your stuff without minimising.
- Don't hold onto things "just in case" you find a future use for them.
- Rent or borrow what you can e.g. a carpet shampooer. Why buy something bulky that will only be used once in a blue moon?
- Don't automatically grab freebies!

- Avoid impulsive buying especially in sales. Remember a bargain is only a bargain if you were intending to buy that product anyway.
- Use the one-in, one-out rule. Whenever you buy something new you need to discard something old.
- Involve other members of the family. You will not be able to discard other people's possessions without their permission so why not have a de-clutter day in which you help each other de-clutter your rooms?
- De-cluttering is not easy. It requires motivation and can be exhausting. But it is tremendously rewarding as maintaining the home becomes much easier and the mind is freed up to focus on more important things, specifically the remembrance of Allah.

LIVE SIMPLY

Prophet Muhammad ﷺ who was the best example to mankind encouraged a life of simplicity stating that *"Simplicity is part of Faith"* (Abu Dawud). He is also reported to have said *"The worldly comforts are not for me. I am like a traveller who takes a rest under a tree in the shade and then goes on his way"* (Tirmidhi).

We should ask ourselves: are we really following the example of our beloved Prophet ﷺ? Are we living like travellers or has the culture of consumerism distracted us from the true purpose of our life which is to worship Allah? In fact we have become so concerned about the comforts of this life and about acquiring more wealth and material goods that we are failing to prepare for the everlasting Akhirah. And how much is enough? People take out loans to buy bigger houses and better cars but there is always another latest gadget coming out or an even bigger home or car to be pursued. The appetite is insatiable. This is why Prophet Muhammad ﷺ said: *"If a son of Adam were to own a valley full of gold, he would desire to have two. Nothing can fill his belly except the earth (of the grave). Allah turns with mercy to him who turns to Him in repentance"* (Al-Bukhari: 444).

At the end of the day it is still possible to live life simply and encourage others to do the same. The following is a real-life conversation that took place in a recent "Family Retreat" event for Muslims in Nottingham, UK. Two women were browsing the hijab/jilbab stalls at the event (their names have been changed).

Safia:	"Gosh there are so many lovely designs to choose from, you feel you have to buy something!"
Jawairia (smiles):	"I don't really feel tempted. I have one coat, one handbag and one pair of shoes. That's enough for me."
Safia (surprised):	"That's amazing. My grandmother used to live like that. She loved simplicity and would give away anything she didn't use. She died in a state of sujud in front of the Kabah."
Jawairia:	"Subhanallah!"

RECLAIM YOUR TIME AND USE IT EFFECTIVELY

Time in the life of a Muslim is a precious blessing. We are told to take advantage of time while we have it, and to use it wisely. We all have a finite number of days in this life in which to gain the pleasure of Allah, seek His forgiveness and ensure that our good deeds weigh heavily on our scales on the Day of Judgement. The importance of time is  encapsulated in one of the shortest Surahs of the Quran, Surat Al-Asr (103). Allah Almighty swears by time that most people are in a state of loss (because they are not using their time in the best way). However the successful people are those who have faith, do righteous deeds and remind each other about what is right and about patience.

We are living in the age of technology which has provided us with numerous benefits. However it has also led to us wasting an unprecedented amount of time in entertainment, surfing the net and engaging in social media. We need to reclaim the unlimited hours we are losing on our smartphones and devices and occupy ourselves with more worthwhile things that benefit us and others in the Dunya and the Akhirah.

How to have Barakah (blessing) in your time

- Sleep early and then take advantage of the blessings of early morning for our work and provision. The Prophet ﷺ made Dua: *"O Allah bless my nation in their early mornings"* (Ibn Majah).

- As Muslims we have been gifted with Salah. The fixed times of Salah enable us to structure our day so that as well as praying punctually we are able to co-ordinate our daily tasks with our worship. This improves time efficiency.

- Develop spirituality and closeness to Allah through allocating specific times in the day for other forms of worship; e.g. recitation/ contemplation of the Quran, Dhikr and Dua. The Quran and hadith provide recommended times for various acts of worship.

- Make a menu planner for a week or a fortnight and shop accordingly. This ensures that you will not waste time constantly agonising over what to cook for dinner. You don't have to stick to it rigidly but it still lists plenty of ideas for meals. Similarly plan ahead for packed lunches.

- Plan for the day ahead. Decide (and iron) what you will wear the next day.

- If you have an appointment aim to reach there ten minutes early. This means you are unlikely to be late and you will arrive calm and collected for your appointment. If you are running late it is polite to inform the other parties.

- Prioritise time for people around you: your parents, spouse, children and others.

- Be more organised. This will give you a clear vision of what you want to get done and you will allow yourself enough time and energy to complete the tasks. Once completed your time will be freed up and you can relax without having to worry about unfinished work.

- Learn to overcome procrastination. This is one of the most valuable life skills we can have. The sooner you can get something done the better.
- Create To-Do-Lists and have the satisfaction of ticking off tasks as you complete them.
- Don't get distracted. Your time is valuable and it is up to you to protect it.
- When you drift along without a clear focus or plan it is so much easier to waste time or even be tempted to sin. It is vital to have direction and purpose in life.
- Make Dua to Allah for Barakah in your time. Good time management significantly improves your wellbeing.

Chapter 9

10· Wellbeing in the Life After Death

Belief in life after death is an essential concept of Islam. We are taught that this life is a test and is temporary, but the Hereafter is eternal. We are all responsible for our actions and on the Day of Judgement our record of deeds will be presented to us so that we can be questioned about the life we led. So our most important goal in life should be to prepare ourselves for the Hereafter by leading a life in obedience to Allah and by performing deeds that are pleasing to Him. How can we prepare ourselves for our journey into the Hereafter?

RECITATION OF THE QURAN

Regular recitation and contemplation of the Quran is one of the best ways to gain the pleasure of Allah. Some Surahs are of particular benefit to us for the Hereafter; e.g. Surah Mulk. Recitation of Surah Mulk every night is a protection for us from the punishment of the Grave. It was narrated that Abd-Allah ibn Masud 🙵 said: "Whoever reads *Tabarak alladhi bi yadihi'l-mulk* [i.e. Surah al-Mulk] every night, Allah will protect him from the torment of the grave. At the time of the Messenger of Allah 🙵 we used to call it al-Mani'ah (that which protects). In the Book of Allah it is a Surah which, whoever recites it every night is duly rewarded" (An-Nasa'i 6:179)

Recite Ayat ul-Kursi after Salah. It was narrated by Abu Umamah 🙵 that "The Messenger of Allah 🙵 said *"Whoever recites Ayat al-Kursi immediately after each prescribed prayer, there will be nothing standing between him and his entering Paradise except death"* (Al-Nasa'i).

INTERCESSION

A significant way to improve our wellbeing in the Hereafter is to discover opportunities through which we can receive intercession on the Day of Judgement. Intercession means mediating for someone else to gain some benefit or ward off harm. The foremost intercessor on that Day will be our beloved Prophet Muhammad 🙵 who has been granted the excellent favour of Intercession for the believers.

The Quran and our fasts will also intercede for us on the Day of Judgement

The Messenger of Allah 🙵 said: *"Fasting and the Quran will intercede on behalf of a person on the Day of Qiyamah. Fasting will say, 'O My Rabb! I prevented him from consuming food and fulfilling his desires so accept my intercession on his behalf.' The Quran will say, 'I prevented him from sleep at night so accept my intercession on his behalf'. Their intercession will be accepted"* (Ahmad).

There are specific surahs in the Quran that can intercede for us on the Day of Judgement

Surah Mulk

It was narrated from Abu Hurayrah ﷺ that the Prophet ﷺ said: *"A Surah from the Quran containing 30 verses will intercede for a man so that he will be forgiven. It is the Surah Tabarak alladhi bi yadihi'l-mulk [i.e. Surah al-Mulk]"* (Al-Tirmidhi: 2891, Abu Dawud: 1400 and Ibn Maajah: 3786).

Surah Baqarah and Surah Al Imran

We are told in the Hadith: *"Recite the Qur'an, for on the Day of Resurrection it will come as an intercessor for those who recite It. Recite the Two Bright Ones, al-Baqarah and Surah Al-Imran, for on the Day of Resurrection they will come as two clouds or two shades, or two flocks of birds in ranks, pleading for those who recite them. Recite Surah al-Baqarah, for to take recourse to it is a blessing and to give it up is a cause of grief, and the magicians cannot confront it"* (Muslim: 804).

Pious muslim friends

In a Hadith narrated by Abu Said al-Khudri ﷺ we are told that when the people of Jannah enter paradise they will question why they don't find their good companions with them. So they will intercede for their friends in front of Allah by saying "O Lord, our brothers used to pray with us and fast with us and do good deeds with us.' Allah will say, 'Go, and whoever you find with an

atom's-weight of faith in his heart, bring him forth. So they will go and bring forth those whom they recognize." (Al-Nisa'i)

This is why it is important to form friendships with pious and righteous people who will not only guide you to do good deeds in this life but will also intercede for you in the next life.

Remind your loved ones to gather enough people to perform your funeral prayer

The Messenger of Allah ﷺ said: *"There is no Muslim who dies and forty men who associate nothing with Allah pray the funeral prayer for him, but Allah will accept their intercession for him"* (Muslim: 1577).

OTHER WAYS TO IMPROVE OUR WELLBEING IN THE HEREAFTER

Our body parts will be a witness for our deeds on the Day of Judgement

We are told in the Noble Quran that "This Day, We shall seal up their mouths, and their hands will speak to Us, and their legs will bear witness to what they used to earn" (36:65). So in order to abide by the commands of Allah, attain His mercy and avoid His wrath it is of vital importance to abstain from all the sins involving various parts of our body.

Settle any disputes with other people before you die

Abu Said al-Khudri reports that the Prophet said, "When the believers cross the Hellfire, they will be stopped at a small arched bridge (Qantarah) before entering the paradise and will be given retribution for injustices between them until they become purified. (Then) they will be permitted to enter Jannah. So, by the One in Whose Hands is my soul, they will know their way to their homes in Jannah, better than they know their ways to their homes in Dunya" (Al-Bukhari).

> Al-Qantarah is a small bridge after the Sirat that the believers will have to cross before entering Jannah. Allah will ask the believers to settle their disputes here.

Imagine a person standing at the Qantarah, right before the gates of Jannah. But they are prevented from entering because they have unresolved issues with other people. Surely it is better to settle all disputes while we are alive so we can depart from this world in a state of purification. If we have expectations of Allah's mercy and forgiveness on the Day of Judgement should we not be forgiving and reconciling with each other in this life?

SADAQAH JAARIYAH

Not only is it important for us to prepare for our journey to the Akirah, which begins with death but we should also ensure that what we leave behind in the world benefits us after we have departed. Abu Hurairah ﷺ reported: The Messenger of Allah ﷺ said *"When a man dies his deeds come to an end except for three: A continuous charity, knowledge by which people derive benefit and a pious child who prays for him"* (Muslim).

A recurring charity or Sadaqah Jaariyah, brings reward to the giver even after his death so long as his charity continues to help and benefit others. Examples of Sadaqah Jaariyah are building a well, sponsoring and educating a child, building a Madrassa or masjid and planting a tree.

TO LEAVE BEHIND BENEFICIAL KNOWLEDGE

- Donate towards the printing and distribution of the Quran or Islamic books.
- Share Islamic videos including lectures and courses that people

can learn and benefit from.
- Write articles, blogs and books so you can impart your knowledge and help people become better Muslims.

RAISE PIOUS CHILDREN

Whatever efforts we put in as Muslim parents to raise our children are an investment for us and will benefit us in this world and in the Hereafter. The Messenger of Allah ﷺ said: *"The one who guides to something good has a reward similar to that of its doer"* (Muslim). Thus if we give our children the right tarbiyyah (training) according to the teachings of Islam they will serve as an on-going charity (Sadaqa Jariyyah) for us even after our departure from this world and we shall be continuously receiving rewards of their righteous actions and Duas while we are in our graves.

WRITE A WILL

Our beloved Prophet ﷺ is reported to have said *"It is the duty of a Muslim who has anything to bequest not to let two nights pass without writing a will about it"* (Al-Bukhari).

Why is it so essential to make a will?

Dividing your estate according to the rules outlined in the Holy Quran is an act of obedience to Allah and hence rewarded by Him. It makes financial sense. If you die intestate (i.e. without making a will) your wealth will be distributed according to English law which will be entirely different to Sharia. Additionally a will can help reduce the amount of Inheritance tax that might be payable on your property and wealth after you pass away. Writing a will gives you peace of mind and makes it much easier for your family and loved ones to sort out your finances when you die. Unnecessary running around, additional expenses and family disputes can be avoided. If children under the age of eighteen lose both their parents the Courts may make the decision as to who takes care of them. By writing a will you can state who should have guardianship of your children if (Allah forbid) the unthinkable happens. You can specify your funeral and burial arrangements, eg.

- not having a post mortem done on your body.
- having a burial without a coffin.
- having a Muslim burial without un-Islamic rituals that are innovations (Bid'ah).
- stating where you wish to be buried.

As mentioned above making a will ensures correct distribution of your wealth according to the fixed shares that are specified in the Quran. Writing an Islamic will is not difficult- quite often people will simply state they want their estate to be divided amongst their family "according to Sharia"  without stipulating exact amounts. For those who wish to write their own wills there are Sharia compliant will templates available online but it is a good idea to seek advice from a Muslim solicitor who specialises in Islamic wills.

Islamic law allows a person to leave up to one third of his wealth to anyone he wishes. He has to clearly specify this in his will. He may choose to support charities so he continues to gain reward after his death.

Remember that according to British law you will need to sign your will in the presence of two witnesses, who will then counter sign. It is also important to update your will regularly as your circumstances change.

It is also an opportunity for him to help friends or family who are not entitled to inherit his money from the fixed shares of Sharia.

A note about Gifts

Wealth that is willingly given away whilst one is alive is regarded as a Gift and does not follow the same rulings as an Islamic will. However it is important to remember that children must be treated fairly and it is not permissible for a person to gift wealth to some of his children and not to others.

SOME SPECIFIC DUAS FOR THE HEREAFTER

رَبَّنَآ اِنَّنَآ اٰمَنَّا فَاغْفِرْ لَنَا ذُنُوْبَنَا وَقِنَا عَذَابَ النَّارِ

- "Rabbana innana amanna faghfir lana dhunuubana wa qinna 'adhaban-Naar (Our Lord! We have indeed believed, so forgive us our sins and save us from the punishment of the Fire)" (3:16).

ربنا اغفرلي ولوالدي وللمؤمنين يوم يقوم الحساب

- **"Rabbanaghfir lee waliwalidayya walilmu'mineena yawma yaqoomulhisab (O our Lord! cover (us) with Thy Forgiveness- me, my parents, and (all) Believers, on the Day that the Reckoning will be established!)"** (14:41).

اللَّهُمَّ إِنِّي أَعُوذُ بِكَ مِنْ فِتْنَةِ النَّارِ وَعَذَابِ النَّارِ، وَفِتْنَةِ الْقَبْرِ وَعَذَابِ الْقَبْرِ، وَشَرِّ فِتْنَةِ الْغِنَى، وَشَرِّ فِتْنَةِ الْفَقْرِ

- *"Allahumma inni a'udhu bika min fitnatin-nari wa 'adhabin-nar, wa min fitnatil-qabri wa 'adhabil-qabr, wa min sharri fitnatil-ghina wa min sharri fitnatil-faqr (O Allah! I seek refuge with You from the affliction of the Fire, the punishment of the Fire, the affliction of the grave, the punishment of the grave, and the evil of the tribulation of wealth and the evil of the tribulation of poverty)"* (Al-Bukhari).

للَّهُمَّ أَصْلِحْ لِيْ دِيْنِيَ الَّذِيْ هُوَ عِصْمَةُ أَمْرِيْ وَ أَصْلِحْ لِيْ دُنْيَايَ الَّتِيْ فِيْهَا مَعَاشِيْ وَ أَصْلِحْ لِيْ آخِرَتِيَ الَّتِيْ فِيْهَا مَعَادِيْ وَاجْعَلِ الْحَيَاةَ زِيَادَةً لِّيْ فِيْ كُلِّ خَيْرٍ وَّ اجْعَلِ الْمَوْتَ رَاحَةً لِّيْ مِنْ كُلِّ شَرٍّ

- *"Allahumma aslih li dini alladhi huwa 'ismatu amri wa aslih li Dunyaya allati fiha ma'ashi, wa aslih li akhirati allati fiha ma'adi waj'alil hayata ziyadatal li fi kulli khayr waj'alil mawta rahatal li min kulli sharr (O Allah! Rectify for me my Deen which is a means of guarding my matters and my world which is a means of my livelihood, and make good my hereafter in which is my returning, and make my life a means of abundance of all good and my death a means of comfort and peace free from all bad)"* (Muslim).

اَللّٰهُمَّ حَاسِبْنِيْ حِسَا بًا يَّسِيْرًا

- *"Allahumma hasibni hisaban yasiran"* (O Allah, judge me with an easy judgement" (Ahmad).

- It was narrated that Anas said: The Prophet ﷺ said: *"Whoever asks Allah for Paradise three times, Paradise will say, 'O Allah, admit him to Paradise.' Whoever seeks protection from the Fire three times, Hell will say, 'O Allah, protect him from the Fire'"* (Al-Tirmidhi: 2572 and Ibn Majah: 4340).

Chapter 10

11. Treatments Recommended in the Sunnah

In modern day living we are rediscovering therapies and treatments which were practised by the Messenger of Allah ﷺ over fourteen hundred years ago, confirming the fact that they were indeed divine teachings. 'Superfoods' such as honey and olive oil are now recognised as extremely beneficial for our health. We are also realising the significance of spiritual healing through recitation of the Quran and invocations, as well as detoxification through 'hijamah'. It is reassuring to see a growing movement back to natural remedies and the medicine of the Prophet ﷺ.

THE QURAN

Islam offers a comprehensive system to healing, ranging from various laws that determine the overall health of society as well as dietary, spiritual and mental approaches to healing the self. These can be found in the Quran- the final book and the seal of all the revelations of Allah. The evidence for using the Quran for healing is mentioned in the Quran itself where Allah reveals **"We send down (stage by stage) in the Quran that which is a healing and mercy to those who believe"** (17:82).

How does the Quran aid our health and wellbeing?

- It is a book of guidance that is able to provide answers and solutions to the many problems and crises faced by people today.
- When life becomes difficult or we are beset with troubles and grief the Quran lightens our burdens and provides light in our path. When recited in the recommended slow rhythmic tones it is soothing and relaxing to the listener.
- Abiding by the dietery laws in the Quran, e.g. abstaining from alcohol and eating that which is halal, ensures the best possible health benefits for us.
- Surah Al-Fatihah in particular has special blessings as was mentioned by the Prophet ﷺ. In one Hadith the Prophet ﷺ told us that it is *"the Mother of the Quran, the Mother of the Book, the Seven oft-repeated verses and the Great recitation"* (Tirmidhi). This Surah can be used to ward off evil and for general healing.
- Surah Baqarah is the longest Surah in the Quran and we are told in the Hadith that its recitation in a house keeps the Shaytan (Satan) away (Muslim 780).
- The Quran can assist us in performing Ruqyah. This is a spiritual treatment in which a person recites part of the Quran or makes supplication using words recorded in the authentic Hadith of

the Prophet ﷺ. Ruqyah can be used as a means of treating spiritual afflictions (Black magic, Jinn possession and evil eye) along with other illnesses. The most common verses of the Quran recited in Ruqyah are Al-Fatihah and Al-Mu'awidhatayn (last two Surahs of the Quran).

● The Quran is a miracle and a gift to us from Allah. Therefore we need to develop a lasting relationship with the Quran and adhere to its guidance and teaching to help us through life.

HIJAMAH

Hijamah or wet cupping is an ancient therapy whereby toxins and impurities in the blood can be eliminated. This is carried out by using cups to create a tight seal at specific areas of the body. Small incisions are then made in those areas in order to draw out the stagnant blood.

Hijamah was regularly practised by the Prophet ﷺ and he recommended it to his Ummah. It is becoming a popular alternative treatment in our busy and stressed lifestyles. This treatment is useful for pain relief and various diseases as well as delivering stimulating and strengthening effects.

SOME FOODS THAT PROMOTE HEATH AND WELL BEING

Ajwah

The Ajwah is a variety of date commonly found in Arabia, usually slightly smaller than other dates. The Prophet ﷺ recommended this date above other dates. Sa'ad ؓ narrated that he heard the Messenger of Allah ﷺ say *"Whoever takes seven dates in the morning will not be affected by magic or poison that day"* (Al-Bukhari).

Zam Zam water

Zam Zam comes from an underground spring in Mecca and has quenched the thirst of billions of people throughout history, especially during the Hajj pilgrimage. It is extremely pure, free of bacteria and contaminants and contains optimal levels of calcium, magnesium and other minerals. This gives Zam Zam its healing and energising properties. Prophet Muhammad ﷺ recommended the use of Zamzam: *"It is a blessing, and it is food that satisfies"* (Muslim: 4/1922).

Honey

Allah the Almighty states in the Quran "There comes forth from their bellies (of the bees) a drink of varying colour wherein is healing for men. Verily in this is indeed a sign for people who think" (16:68-69).

Prophet Muhammad ﷺ has informed us of the great benefits found in honey. In recent years, scientific research has started supporting the beneficial effects of honey on certain medical and surgical conditions. Honey is a natural, easily digestible and energy rich food which contains carbohydrates, proteins, lipids, enzymes and vitamins. It is effective in treating a host of medical conditions including stomach ailments, coughs/colds, headaches and healing of burns and wounds.

Kalonji (Black Seed)

Abu Hurairah ؓ narrated that the Prophet ﷺ said *"Use the black seed regularly because it is a cure for every disease except death"* (Al-Bukhari and Muslim).

The black seed holds a unique place in the medicine of the Prophet ﷺ and has become very popular with muslims as well as non-Muslims. Kalonji and its oil has many healing properties against ailments such as migraines, colds, asthma, skin disorders and respiratory diseases. It also benefits the stomach and helps the body build resistance against disease.

Olive oil

Umar ibn al-Khattab ؓ narrated that he heard the Prophet ﷺ say *"Consume Olive oil and anoint yourself with it for indeed it is from a blessed tree"* (Al-Tirmidhi).

Extra virgin olive oil is rich in healthy monounsaturated fats, as well as containing large amounts of antioxidants. Its strong anti-inflammatory properties mean that it can reduce the risk of major diseases such as cancer, heart disease, diabetes, arthritis and Alzheimer's.

Milk

Milk is rich in nutrients such as calcium, phosphorus, magnesium and riboflavin. It aids the development of strong bones and teeth and also promotes the growth of healthy muscle. Milk was one of the preferred drinks of the Messenger of Allah ﷺ because based on a Hadith related by Imam Tirmidhi the Prophet ﷺ said that nothing suffices as food and drink except milk.

Vinegar

Long before scientific research proved its health benefits Prophet Muhammad ﷺ recommended vinegar as a food that is preferable and good for us. As reported by Jabir ؓ: *"I entered the house of the Prophet ﷺ with him and there was some bread and vinegar. The Messenger of Allah ﷺ said: 'Eat; what a good condiment is vinegar'"* (An- Nasa'i: 3796).

Apple Cider Vinegar in particular has numerous health benefits. It is an effective digestive cleansing agent and helps control blood glucose levels for those suffering from diabetes. There are other uses of vinegar as a remedy for specific illnesses and conditions:

- It is a good source of polyphenols which help prevent heart disease, osteoporosis cancer and diabetes.
- Lowers cholesterol
- Regulates blood pressure
- Soothes sore throat and helps clear congestion
- Boosts energy
- Aids weight loss

It is significant to note that although these products hold numerous benefits and cures, the only true cure is from Allah and He cures when and how He desires. Often someone taking the products prescribed by the Prophet ﷺ may feel their condition has not improved at all or has further deteriorated. This does not in any way mean that these products do not have a benefit but rather at such times we should remember that Shifa (cure) is only in the hands of Allah. We should pray to Allah that He cures us just as the Prophet ﷺ was cured by consuming certain products.

SEEK PROFESSIONAL HELP WHERE NEEDED

Muslims are encouraged to explore and use both traditional and modern forms of medicine. The treatments mentioned in this chapter are not intended to be a substitute for professional medical advice or treatment. Remember to seek the advice of your GP or other health professional regarding any medical condition that you may have or that you may be concerned about. It is important to take action where necessary as well as putting your trust in Allah: Anas ibn Malik ﷺ reported: *A man said, "O Messenger of Allah, should I tie my camel and trust in Allah, or should I leave her untied and trust in Allah?" The Messenger of Allah ﷺ said, "Tie her and trust in Allah"* (Al-Tirmidhi: 2517).

We should also bear in mind that illness is not always an affliction. Rather it is a test from Allah to identify if his servant can remain patient and steadfast through times of adversity. We have been taught that whoever is patient at such times will reap great rewards. Allah states in the Quran: "O you who believe, seek assistance through patience and prayer; surely Allah is with the patient" (2:153).

12. Duas for Protection and Wellbeing

DUA AT THE TIME OF DIFFICULTY OR DISTRESS

The Messenger of Allah ﷺ used to say when he was in distress:

لا إله إلا الله العظيم الحليم، لا إله إلا الله رب العرش العظيم، لا إله إلا الله رب السماوات ورب الأرض ورب العرش الكريم

"La ilaha illallahul-Azimul-Halim. La ilaha illallahu Rabbul-'Arshil-'Azim. La ilaha illallahu Rabbus-samawati, wa Rabbul-ardi, wa Rabbul-'Arshil- Karim (None has the right to be worshipped but Allah the Incomparably Great, the Compassionate. None has the right to be worshipped but Allah the Lord of the Mighty Throne. None has the right to be worshipped but Allah the Lord of the heavens, the Lord of the earth, and the Lord of the Honourable Throne)" (Al-Bukhari and Muslim).

PROTECTION FROM SHAYTAN

There are many ways of protecting ourselves and our homes from Shaytan.

Protection of our homes

Abu Hurairah ﷺ reported that the Messenger of Allah ﷺ said *"Do not turn your houses into graveyards. Satan runs away from the house in which Surah Al-Baqarah is recited"* (Muslim: 780).

What to say when leaving the home

بِسْمِ اللهِ، تَوَكَّلْتُ عَلَى اللهِ، وَلَا حَوْلَ وَلَا قُوَّةَ إِلَّا بِاللهِ

"Bismillaahi, tawakkaltu 'alallaahi, wa laa hawla wa laa quwwata 'illa billaah (In the Name of Allah, I have placed my trust in Allah, there is no might and no power except by Allah)" (Abu Dawud: 5095).

What to say when entering the home

بِسْمِ اللهِ وَلَجْنَا، وَ بِسْمِ اللهِ خَرَجْنَا، وَعَلَى رَبِّنَا تَوَكَّلْنَا

"Bismillaahi walajnaa, wa bismillaahi kharajnaa, wa 'alaaRabblnaa tawakkalnaa (In the Name of Allah we enter, in the Name of Allah we leave, and upon our Lord we depend [then say As-Salaamu 'Alaykum to those present])" (Abu Dawud: 5096).

There are Duas for protection, insomnia and seeing bad dreams. These can aid us in getting a good night's sleep which in turn leads to productivity and contributes to good health generally. Restful sleep should also make it easier for us to wake up for Tahajjud and Fajr Salah.

Protection before sleeping

The Prophet ﷺ said: *"By reciting it (Ayat ul-Kursi, Quran 2:255) there will be a guardian appointed over you from Allah who will protect you during the night, and Satan will not be able to come near you until morning"* (Al-Bukhari). The Prophet ﷺ also said *"Whoever recites the last two verses of Surah Al-Baqarah at night, those two verses shall be sufficient for him"* i.e. protect him from all that can cause harm (Bukhari: 5009). It was narrated from A'ishah 🙷 that when the Prophet ﷺ went to bed every night, he would hold his hands together and spittle into them while reciting: *Qul Huwa Allaahu Ahad, Qul a'oodhu bi rabb il-falaq* and *Qul a'oodhu bi rabb il-naas* (the last three Surahs in the Quran) Then he would wipe them over whatever he could of his body, starting with his head and face and the front of his body, and he would do that three times. (Bukhari)

> There are many more Duas that can be recited before sleeping which are to be found in pocket books like *Fortress of a Muslim*. Alternatively they can be downloaded onto phones.

PROTECTION FOR CHILDREN

The Prophet ﷺ used to seek refuge with Allah for al-Hasan 🙷 and al-Husayn 🙷 (His grandsons) with these words:

أُعِيذُكَ بِكَلِمَاتِ اللهِ التَّامَّةِ مِنْ كُلِّ شَيْطَانٍ ، وَهَامَّةٍ ، وَمِنْ كُلِّ عَيْنٍ لَامَّةٍ

"A'oodhu bi kalimaat Allaah al-taammah min kulli shaytaanin wa haammah wa min kulli 'aynin laammah" (I seek refuge in the perfect words of Allah, from every devil and every poisonous reptile, and from every bad eye)" (Al-Bukhari).

PROTECTION AGAINST THE DAJJAL

Al-Maseeh al-Dajjal (the false messiah) will be a man created by Allah to be the greatest fitnah (test) for people at the end of time. He will have the power to travel at phenomenal speed and the ability to perform extraordinary feats like commanding the sky to pour rain and the earth to produce vegetation. Thus he will lead people astray, though the faith of the true believers will be strengthened.

According to a Hadith in Al-Bukhari (6508) he will be a ruddy-complexioned man, well built, with curly hair, blind in his right eye, with his eye looking like a floating grape. Written between his eyes will be "Kaaf-faa'-raa' (K-F-R)", in separate Arabic letters, or "kaafir" (Disbeliever) with the letters joined. This will be read by every Muslim, literate or illiterate.

We should seek refuge with Allah from the fitnah of the Dajjal, especially in Salah (prayer). This has been narrated

Every Prophet warned his Ummah against the one-eyed Dajjal, but Prophet Muhammad ﷺ gave us a clear description of the appearance of Dajjal and how we should protect ourselves from him.

by Umm al-Mu'mineen (Mother of the Believers) 'Aa'ishah ﷺ who said that the Messenger of Allah ﷺ used to pray in his Salah:

اللَّهُمَّ إِنِّي أَعُوذُ بِكَ مِنْ عَذَابِ الْقَبْرِ وَأَعُوذُ بِكَ مِنْ فِتْنَةِ الْمَسِيحِ الدَّجَّالِ وَأَعُوذُ بِكَ مِنْ فِتْنَةِ الْمَحْيَا وَفِتْنَةِ الْمَمَاتِ اللَّهُمَّ إِنِّي أَعُوذُ بِكَ مِنَ الْمَأْثَمِ وَالْمَغْرَمِ

"Allahumma inni a'oodhu bika min 'adhaab al-qabri, wa a'oodhu bika min fitnat il-maseeh il-dajjaal, wa a'oodhu bika min fitnat il-mahyaa wa fitnat il-mamaat. Allahumma inni a'oodhu bika min al-ma'tham wa'l-maghram (O Allah, I seek refuge with You from the torment of the grave, I seek refuge with You from the fitnah of the Dajjal, and I seek refuge with You from the trials of life and death. O Allah, I seek refuge with You from sin and debt)" (Al-Bukhari: 789).

Muslim narrated that Abu Hurairah ﷺ said: The Messenger of Allah ﷺ said: *"When any one of you says Tashahhud, let him seek refuge with Allah from four things, and say:*

اللَّهُمَّ إِنِّي أَعُوذُ بِكَ مِنْ عَذَابِ جَهَنَّمَ وَمِنْ عَذَابِ الْقَبْرِ وَمِنْ فِتْنَةِ الْمَحْيَا وَالْمَمَاتِ وَمِنْ شَرِّ فِتْنَةِ الْمَسِيحِ الدَّجَّالِ

'Allahumma inni a'oodhi bika min 'adhaab jahannam wa min 'adhaab al-qabri wa min fitnat il-mahyaa wa'l-mamaat wa min sharri fitnat al-maseeh al-dajjaal (O Allah, I seek refuge with You from the torment of Hell, from the torment of the grave, from the trials of life and death, and from the evil of the fitnah of the Dajjal)" (Muslim: 924).

Abu Darda ﷺ reported Allah's Prophet ﷺ as saying: *"If anyone learns by heart the first ten verses of the Surah al-Kahf he will be protected from the Dajjal"* (Muslim: 4/1766).

DUAS FOR WELLBEING

اللَّهُمَّ إِنِّي أَسْأَلُكَ الْعَافِيَة

"Allahumma inni as' aluka al'afiyah (O Allah, I ask you for Afiyah (wellbeing)" (Tirmidhi).

اللهم إني أسألك الهدى، والتقى، والعفاف، والغنى

"Allahumma inni as'alukal-huda, wat-tuqa, wal-'afafa, wal-ghina(O Allah! I beseech You for guidance, piety, chastity and prosperity)" (Muslim).

للَّهُمَّ إِنِّي أَسْأَلُكَ عِلْمًا نَافِعًا وَ رِزْقًا طَيِّبًا وَ عَمَلاً مُتَقَبَّلاً

"Allahumma inni as'aluka 'Ilman naafi'an, wa rizqan tayyiban, wa 'amalan mutaqabbalan (Allah! I ask You for knowledge that is of benefit, a good provision and deeds that will be accepted)" (Ibn Majah).

The following Dua was one that the Prophet of Allah ﷺ used to say in abundance:

رَبَّنَآ ءَاتِنَا فِى ٱلدُّنْيَا حَسَنَةً وَفِى ٱلْأَخِرَةِ حَسَنَةً وَقِنَا عَذَابَ ٱلنَّارِ

"Rabbanaaa aatinaa fid-Dunyaa Hasanatan wa fil-aakhirati Hasanatan wa qinaa 'adhaab-an-naar (Our Lord! Give us in this world that which is good and in the Hereafter that which is good, and save us from the torment of the Hell Fire!)" (Surah Al-Baqarah: 2:201)

اللهُمَّ أَصْلِحْ لِي دِينِي الَّذِي هُوَ عِصْمَةُ أَمْرِي، وَأَصْلِحْ لِي دُنْيَايَ الَّتِي فِيهَا مَعَاشِي، وَأَصْلِحْ لِي آخِرَتِي الَّتِي فِيهَا مَعَادِي، وَاجْعَلِ الْحَيَاةَ زِيَادَةً لِي فِي كُلِّ خَيْرٍ، وَاجْعَلِ الْمَوْتَ رَاحَةً لِي مِنْ كُلِّ شَرٍّ

"Allahumma aslih li dini alladhi huwa 'ismatu amri wa aslih li Dunyaya allati fiha ma'ashi, wa aslih li akhirati allati fiha ma'adi waj'alil hayata ziyadatal li fi kulli khayr waj'alil mawta rahatal li min kulli sharr (O Allah, rectify my religion which is the safeguard of my affairs, rectify my worldly life in which is my livelihood, and rectify my Hereafter which is my place of return. Make life a source of abundance of every good and make my death a relief and comfort from every evil)" (Muslim: 2720)

Chapter 12

13. Closing Remarks

We seek help from Allah and depend on Him alone. There is neither might nor power except with Allah, the Almighty. O Allah, send prayers and salutations and blessings on Muhammad, his family, his Companions and those who follow in his footsteps. And all praise is for Allah, Lord of the worlds.

May Allah forgive me if I have made any errors in my book. If I have said anything wrong then know that it is either from the Shaytan or my own self, and if I have said anything good, then know that it is from Allah.

Please remember my family and the Ummah in your Duas. May Allah bless us all with excellent health and wellbeing as well as khair in our deeds and intentions. May Allah grant us all Jannat ul-Firdaws and protect us from the punishment of the fire and the grave. Ameen.

Acknowledgements

First and foremost I would like to thank Allah the Almighty. In the process of putting this book together I realised that He has gifted me with the ability to write and the determination to pursue my dreams.

I would like to offer special thanks to Hafidh Wahid, Director of Darussalam Publishing, London for accepting my manuscript and giving me the unique opportunity of having my book published.

My thanks are also extended to Brother Azhar Majothi, Manager of Ihsaan Design, Leicester for his professional editing and design of my book.

My deep and sincere gratitude to my husband for supporting me in spreading beneficial knowledge and for looking after us in every way.

Thank you to my three amazing and beautiful children who are always good company. May Allah bless them with wonderful lives.

Last but not least I am grateful to my mother for the training and life skills that she gave me to navigate through life.

NOTES

NOTES

NOTES

NOTES